As a Man Drinketh

A (Mostly) Useful Guide
for Mending a Man's Mind

Copyright

Dedicated to my wonderful wife, Jessica, and to my cherished children, Kyler, Chandra, Kali, and Lokelani…

I'm sorry. Please forgive me. Thank you.

I love you.

Acknowledgements

Without receiving some serious help from a shitload of people, this book never would've made it out of my weird, wild and crazy mind. To all those who've offered me help, support, and a hand-up over the years – even when I didn't necessarily deserve it – thank you from all of my heart. If it weren't for you fine and fabulous folks and the positive impact you had in my life, there wouldn't be a book for me to write. And there might not have even been a me around to write it.

My Creator; My wife Jessica and my children Kyler, Chandra, Kali and Lokelani; The Arnett's: Mom, Dad, Sean, Lauri, Jason, Amy, Ryan, Aaron, Shana, Sabrina, Eamon, April, and Jaime; All my nieces and nephews; My Texas Fam: Uncle Greg, Aunt Mary, Amanda, Ellen, James, Uncle Bubba, Aunt Yo, Shane, Jonathan, William, Natalie Martinez-Long, and Miriam Wasilewski; My in-laws (Millet): Gary, Marsha, Dave, Alex, Uncle Blaine, Aunt Lorrie, and Duke; My son's mama: Kristy Minnick-Maclure; My brothers from another mother who had an awesome impact in my life: Cory Tsouras, Jared Gilthorpe, Dean Howell, Nathan Levinson, Blake Child, Dwyer McDuffee, Breck Edwards, Tyson "Son of Ty" Ennis, Adam "GOAT" Densely, Matt "Tex" Ludlow, Casey "C-Hutch" Hutchens, Steven "Steve-O" Fisher, Jay Odom, Brad Mahana, Casey Baker, Chris Levinson, Zackery Wright, Jared McWilliams, Christopher Allen, Caleb Cole, Scott Friedeck, Aaron Bush, Mike "Mikey" Jeppson, Davin Birdwell, Jason Williamson, Joey Manuel, Dallon Garrett, Eddie Kloesel, Owen Gross, Justin Ward, Adam "Flow-State" Bramlage, Christopher Stubbs, Brandon Duncan, Jonathan Hill, Mike Collings, Randall Corcoran, Jody Clegg, Omar

Abou-Ismail, Brandon Rowe, and Colby Draper; My sisters from another mister: Annie Pearson, Jenny Wade-Weilacher, Rachel "Rancho" Bagwell-Means, Natasha Wojtowich-Smith, Jennifer McDuffee, Kat Child, Felicia Giouzelis, and Jessica Saucier; My Hawaii Ohana: Steven Kalish, Patrick Burke, Juli Anderson, Dana Premanandi, Jenny Bach, Uncle Bully, Antonio Priola, Cory Michaud, and Robert Young; The entire Elsmore and Boyakin clan; My former girlfriends; All my social media MENtors (men I follow and recommend following, all of whom had some measure of positive impact on my life, if even a virtual one): Sean Whalen, Garrett J. White, Dan Meredith, Ryan Stewman, Jesse Elder, Rob Bailey, Ryan Michler, Setema Gali, Jon Paramore, Garrain Jones, Gary Vaynerchuk, , Chadd Wright, Dan Fleyshman, Mark Evans, Kyler "The Captain" Creek, Jason Wilson, Tim Ballard, Rob Dyrdek, The Liver King, Zuby, Paul Stamets, Novak Djokovic, Tim Tebow, Ian Smith, Tommy Vext, David "Avocado" Wolfe, Jesse Itzler, David Goggins, Brad Lea, Tim Grover, Dan Young, Aaron Wagner, Jimmy Rex, Andy Frisella, Ed Mylett, Dr. Joe Dispenza, MrBallen, and a special posthumous shoutout to Neal Currey.

And last but never least: Me, Myself, and I, Bryce Trevor Arnett.

Thank you for blessing my life with your presence alone.

Much Love,

Bryce, B-Rice, B-Rizzle, Brizzly Bear

Contents

Introduction

I am ready to face any challenges that might be foolish enough to face me.

–Dwight K. Schrute

As a Man Drinketh took me over 40 years to write. To put that in perspective, I'm 40 years young right now and it's 2022 – so yeah, essentially my entire fucking existence here on Earth. Forty. Fucking. Years. Sheesh.

Sure, I'm still a baby by some standards – and this book didn't *literally* take me four decades to pen – however, it *did* take me 30 of those 40 years to see how far I could push the absolute outer-limits of my capacity for self-sabotage, just so I had enough material to write about.

In other words, I worked really hard at fucking up my life… on my own… with no one else to blame, to help me out, or for me to pin my shit on.

But the good news is that I didn't FUBAR my life. That's Fuck Up Beyond All Recognition, for those who are wondering. Instead, I managed to turn it around, despite my penchant for pissing it away. And during those decades of despair, I snagged a nugget of wisdom or two, a few stone-cold truths and even some psychedelically enhanced downloads along my path to self-improvement and self-discovery.

1

And while I'm still on that path – and *will be* until my last breath, because the path to inner-fulfillment is a lifetime trek – I feel a duty and responsibility to deliver those inspirations, wisdoms, (and above all else), warnings, to all the men who feel like they could use an honest dose of reality – coupled with some sympathetic compassion – from a man who's been through the depths of hell within his own mind.

A man like yours truly.

A man who's lied to everyone, including himself. A man who's been a thieving criminal. A man who's manipulated and cheated others. A man who's been to jail. A man who's been homeless. A man who got his girlfriend pregnant in high school. A man who abandoned his kid and became a deadbeat dad. A man with a shitty dad himself. A man with a dysfunctional family dynamic. A man who's stolen too many things to count, including his best friend's truck.

A man who has battled crippling depression, anxiety and self-doubt since childhood. A man who's thought about or attempted suicide by overdosing on pills or by driving his girlfriend's car into a concrete median on the freeway. A man who's struggled with self-medicating through painkillers, crank, cocaine, SSRIs, benzos, sleeping pills, marijuana, nicotine, caffeine, soda, sugar, hardcore drinking, porn, and sex, just to name a few.

A man who has a wife and kids and came within an inch of losing his life and family because he was *that* fucked up in his own head.

A man like yours truly.

This book is a collection of my life experiences over the past few decades. It is what I learned about myself through the art of self-sabotage, bouts of depression, addiction, self-doubt, feelings of worthlessness, thoughts of suicide, and a whole host of other mental, emotional, and spiritual issues.

As I near 3 years of sobriety from a vicious, 12-year alcohol addiction, what I have uncovered about my mind and the true origin of my problems has been life-altering. And I wish to share my wisdoms with all the men who are struggling to hang on, including you. Because brother, I've been there too – feeling hopeless and like there's no other way out – and I **know** you can be right where I am as well. But not without some serious self-realization and some seriously hard fucking work first.

Many of the topics in this book will seem repetitive or redundant. That's because they are. I intentionally did that and mention certain things several times (and in several different ways) because not everyone learns the same way or the first time they're presented with something. These were the keys to unlocking my potential, to me getting (and staying) sober, and to me finally freeing myself from the fucked-up prison of my mind.

These were the lifelines that gave my weakened mind the shred of strength needed to pull myself up and out of the darkest, deepest, dankest, most depressing mental hellhole imaginable. These keys helped me take full responsibility for my life. They were the gifts given to me by God.

This book is me reciprocating those gifts with a humble heart, by paying it forward to you and back to all the men out there who have offered me a hand-up along the way. The friends, the father-figures, and especially the antagonists. I am grateful for you all.

And I am grateful for you, the reader. I promise I won't give up on you. Thank you for being here.

Now let's fucking GO!!

Stop Fucking Lying

The best place to start is by telling the fucking truth.
−Sean Whalen

True freedom can only be found in the mind. And it only comes when you free yourself from the lies that keep you imprisoned behind bars, trapped in a cell of your own making. It comes when you force yourself to stop running from the truth and not only face that self-made shitstorm behind you, but turnabout and sprint *towards* it with your chin up and your chest out.

Freedom comes when you stop giving a shit what all the meaningless dicks and d-bags of the world think. The *instant* you realize you've been wasting your precious fucks on the wrong things in life and start focusing your time and energy on doling out all the *right* ones instead − that there, my friend, is when your freedom begins. That there is your Independence Day.

So what are you waiting for? For a wake-up call? For permission? This book is your wakeup call, brother, and this is me giving you permission to let freedom ring. Because you are the most precious fuck of all. The naysayers haven't the faintest idea who you really are, and they haven't the first fucking clue who you were born to be.

You're afraid that those who love and support you won't anymore if they know who you *really* are, what you've *really* done. You're scared to tell the truth and that's understandable, because that means exposing yourself and admitting you've been living a lie. It means risking what you have. That means it may cost you relationships. That means it *will* cost you your (old) life. You can't have everything you want unless you're willing to risk what you have now.

But aren't you tired of feeling like a prisoner in your own mind? Tired of living a life sentence?

Well brother, the only way to free yourself from the prison that keeps you chained to your past is to tell the truth about it. All of it. Every dirty little detail. To yourself. To your family. To your wife and/or kids. All of it. Don't hold back. Share that shit.

You're in a hard place right now. I get that. I'm sympathetic to your plights. If I wasn't, this book wouldn't exist. Nevertheless, it's time for you to stop fucking around and to start being the man you were born to be. So please stop lying to yourself and start bearing the fucking truth.

You need to stop lying. Stop lying to friends and family. Stop lying to society and on social media. But more importantly than that, you need to stop lying to yourself.

I repeat: Stop Fucking Lying. Get honest. Radically honest. Honest about who you are. Honest about your past. Honest about what you're going through right now. *Especially* about what you're going through right now.

So here's my first suggestion of the book: get radically honest with yourself. Take inventory of the lies you have told and the lies you are perpetuating. Come clean to yourself first, and then to those around you.

Why? Because I did it, and because I'm sharing my shit now, in this book. And I won't ask, suggest or advise you to do anything I haven't done myself first. No foundation can withstand mistrust. Nothing good can form from lies. Now go get honest with yourself and the world. It's time to shine.

Never-Ending (Victim) Story

You can't expect to be a victor if you're living with a victim mentality.

–Billy Cox

Should this book have found its way into your hands, then it's safe for me to assume that your mindset might be a tad dysfunctional and maybe you're having a hard time coping with life in general.

Maybe you're struggling with depression, PTSD or some other issue that is quickly deteriorating your mental health. Maybe you're dealing with a hard-core addiction, like I did. But even if you aren't dealing with any of those things, I'm going to go ahead and suggest that you are likely addicted to something and may not even realize it.

That addiction is called your victim story. You are addicted to being a victim. You're trapped in a perpetual cycle of self-suffering – where you choose to play both the victim *and* the victimizer – and where none of it is ever your fault. Now I can hear you thinking "I'm not addicted to victimhood" and I'm going to have to go ahead and call bullshit on your ass.

I only became aware of my addiction to self-pity a couple of years ago. My never-ending victim story was deep-rooted and the source from which all of my substance abuse problems started. But it was hard for me to see it.

When you're trapped in that "poor me/why me?" state of mind, like I was, you can literally rationalize the most ridiculous behavior and blame it on whom or whatever you want. Sound familiar? And that victim in your mind will not only condone your bullshit behavior, it will *encourage* it and even egg you on. My personal favorite sob story was, "I didn't drink until I met my wife."

Ugh. Sometimes I wish I could go back in time and kick my own ass, but then I realize that that douchebag wasn't even the real me. Instead of feeling angry about who I used to be, I've learned to forgive that guy because he was trapped in the victim mentality. That's a shitty place to be. Now, I just feel for that poor, drunk fucker.

Do you want to continue to be a victim? Victims blame others for their plights, believing the world is out to get them. Victims live with trauma. They lack healthy coping mechanisms and boundaries. They can find a problem for every solution. They lack self-confidence and personal conviction. They feel powerless and are often angry, frustrated, and resentful. And last, but not least, they engage in negative self-talk and self-sabotage. In other words: *Victims are their own worst enemies.*

Or do you want to cross the bridge of personal responsibility and become a victor? Victors see themselves as their ultimate ally and see every situation (whether a success or a failure) as an opportunity to grow and evolve. Victors are problem solvers. Victors grow from their traumas and find a way to help others get through theirs. Victors think and speak kindly to themselves, supporting themselves as they climb the ladder of personal fulfillment.

Brother, I know you weren't born to wallow in self-pity. But I also know how hard it can be to break free from that mindset. Fortunately for you, you have *me* and this book, which I wrote specifically to support you in killing the victim within.

Now let's bury that bastard once and for all.

The Solution is You

Uncomfortable truth: 90% of the problems in your life are directly your fault and 100% of them are your responsibility to fix—your fault or not.

–Ian Smith

The addiction to my victim mentality might've been harder to beat than my addiction to booze. It certainly lasted longer. For years and years I blamed my parents for sandbagging my potential for success. Then I blamed my girlfriend for my failures when she got pregnant in high school. Then I blamed the drugs, then my wife, then the alcohol, then my kids, and then society.

And finally, when I decided to kill myself, I put **all** the blame on the Man Above: God. But none of that blame got me any closer to turning my life around.

As I started to work on mending my mental health and began framing a brand-new mindset, it dawned on me that there really was no one else to pin my problems on except me, myself, and I.

The cold-hard truth that most men refuse to accept is that the world is reacting and responding to you with whatever energy you have sent out. In other words, you are reaping what you've sown.

Life is reciprocal and shit isn't happening *to* you, it's happening *for* you and *because* of you. You don't want to accept responsibility for the problems in your life because most – if not *all* – of the problems you are facing are a direct result of your actions (or inactions).

Not doing something is still doing something, even if it doesn't seem like it. It's called COI or Cost of Inaction and it's the return on investment you're getting for not making decisions, whether you like it or not.

A big step in changing your mind and life is being willing to accept responsibility for where you are (rather than blaming others), regardless of how "severe" the situation may appear on the outside. *All* of your problems – not some, mind you, but every-single-one of them – are **yours** to fix, whether you caused them or not. Read that again.

Sometimes you may be forced to do something, but *no one* is forced into a victim's perspective. Only you can choose to see life through the victim mindset. And only *you* can choose to change that.

Now I don't know you and I don't know your problems but the solution is the same, brother: *it's you*. And there's isn't a book (this one included) that can help you realize that, unless you're prepared to put aside your pride and ego.

When you drop the pride, stop blaming others (people, things, situations, etc), and take responsibility for your life, you become your own solution. It is then, through you, that your own problems can be solved and transmuted into opportunities.

At the end of the day the buck stops with you. No one is coming to save you. *You* are the one you have been waiting for.

One More Day

The epic story of tomorrow can't be written if it ends today.
                                                    –Unknown

Men are offing themselves at an alarming rate, worldwide and across all demographics. I'd cite the statistics here but it's too tragic and you can research that shit on your own. I'll just leave it at this - the numbers ain't good.

If you're reading this right now and you're having thoughts about killing or harming yourself, brother **please** reach out to someone who can offer you support. Anyone. Don't let your sadness die within you.

Let me preface the rest of this chapter by saying that there is no shame in admitting that you've thought about doing it before, or in being open about the times you've actually tried. I've been there before. Every-so-often an unexpected question pops into my mind, wondering whether my wife and kids would be better off without me.

I've considered ending my own life and thought of suicide countless times since I was a first diagnosed with depression as a teenager. I've actually attempted to kill myself a few times too. I feel **zero** fucking shame in admitting that.

I downed a few bottles of sleeping pills because the pain from a broken heart was too much to handle. One time I took

14

my then-girlfriend's car and deliberately loosened the lug nuts in the hope that the tires would fall off. And when that didn't work fast enough, I took the car and smashed it into the median on the freeway. More recently, I would take my handgun, rack it, then stick the barrel in my mouth and start squeezing the trigger, wondering how much pressure it'd take before BANG!, lights out.

Whatever it is that you are going through now is temporary. I know that's an oversimplification of an incredibly complex issue but trust me, it's temporary. Your life is temporary. The problems you're facing are temporary. What is *not* temporary is the decision to end your life. What is *not* temporary is *you being gone*.

Your problems? Those can be solved. Maybe they can't be solved on your own or right now, but with the help and support of others, trust me my man, together they can be solved.

Even if your life doesn't feel like it's worth anything to you, please believe me when I say it's worth something to those around you. And I may not know you or your problems, but you're genuinely worth something to me. And not just because you're reading my book.

If you are personally struggling with thoughts, feelings, and/or ideations of suicide, please ask for help. Please realize that there are other alternatives to picking a path that obliterates the lives of loved-ones and friends and leaves an abyss that can never be filled, no matter how much time passes.

If you or someone you know is having thoughts of suicide, please dial 988 or call the Suicide and Life Crisis Hotline at 1-800-273-TALK (8255).

Get Back Up Again

Rock bottom became the solid foundation on which I rebuilt my life.

—J.K. Rowling

I don't care who the hell you are, where you're from, or how much bloody money you've got stacked in the bank, you are not immune to falling flat on your fucking face. Rock bottom is an unavoidable and, all-too-often, excruciating part of our existence here on earth.

No matter what, brother, you're going to face peaks and valleys along your path and journey in life. You're going to have highs and lows. Maybe you've hit rock bottom before or you're there right now. But that's actually a good thing.

As someone prone to addiction (who's also had his fair share of mental health challenges) I know all about peaks and valleys. There've been times where I was so high it felt like anything was possible, like my potential was limitless and nothing could stand in my way. Then there've been lows when I've wanted to kill myself and getting out of bed was considered a heroic effort.

There've also been times when I thought I'd hit rock bottom just to have that bottom give out like some portal opened up out of nowhere and I free-fell helplessly to a fresh new level of hell below. And just when I thought *that* was rock bottom… well, you get the idea.

But what I learned during those low times of mine, is that rock bottom doesn't have to happen at your absolute worst. Sometimes the point of impact comes when you can no longer tolerate your shitty situation and you commit to changing it. It comes when you have had enough shit and are willing to accept that you are where you are and it's okay to be there.

Accepting where you are and seeing your part in it is what creates the foundation. It's what allows you to begin building something better.

Many men before us have been curb stomped by life, yet they managed to pick themselves up off the pavement. Take comfort in knowing that you're not alone (nor unique, unfortunately), and that those men left clues you can use to form a foundation of your own. A foundation upon which you can build something new and something greater than ever before.

So if you're at rock bottom right now, just know that it's temporary – but only if you want it to be. And I have a feeling you've had enough. So keep your chin up and chest out and look to the sky above. There's nowhere to go but up.

No Regrets

Not until we are lost do we begin to understand ourselves.
                                        –Henry David Thoreau

This isn't meant to sound like a handicap or a free pass, but you're a dude, dude, and that means you're bound to fuck up and regret something you've done.

You'll regret doing things you wish you hadn't, and you'll even regret *not* doing things you wish you had. You'll feel like a fool for something you said, and you'll curse yourself for not saying something you wish you'd said but didn't because you were too big of pussy to say it.

It's no secret that I've done some dumb shit in my life, hence the book. I've made countless blunders over the past 40 years – some criminal, some not – so having a few regrets here and there comes with the territory. But in the end, what the hell can I do about it now? It's not like I have a plutonium-powered DeLorean or anything. So I've found it's best to leave that shit where it belongs, in my past.

For me, I'm collecting fewer regrets than before because I stopped doing the stupid shit I know I'm going to regret later. Sobriety sure helps, I admit, but I also had to just accept what I'd done and make the choice to ask for forgiveness from those I'd fucked over, forgive myself as well, then move the fuck on. And I've done a lot less stupid shit since then.

19

That's the difference between having regrets and living with them. The past is past. And while it may not be possible to completely forget the past, you don't have to be a slave to it, either. The best thing you can do is learn from your mistakes by doing your best not to repeat them and using those hard-learned lessons as a reference point when you're faced with a similar challenge again. Sounds simple, right?

Shit happens, homie. Risk and regret go hand-in-hand. And it's damn near impossible to avoid regret in life. But you don't have to make it center stage. So please stop giving the greenlight to the skeletons of your past, allowing them to haunt your ass for the rest of your life. Make peace with those old bones then send 'em on to the afterlife, not back into the closet.

If you're going to look back, which you will, then only look long enough to extract the moral or lesson, then turn your ass back around, face forward and keep on moving no matter what.

Jekyll & Hyde

Be yourself; everyone else is already taken.

—Oscar Wilde

Those last few years of my alcohol addiction were pretty shitty for me. Super-duper shitty, honestly. So shitty, in fact, that the best word to describe my overall state of being back then is *sick*. Sick in the body. Sick in the head. Sick emotionally. Sick spiritually. Just. Fucking. Sick. And I was already struggling and somewhat sick in those areas *before* I began drinking, so you can only imagine the compounding effects when you add booze into the equation.

It actually got so bad that my personality altered after just one drink. Hell, it changed with just *one fucking sip*. In fact, toward the end there my wife could **always** tell when I'd been drinking, no matter how hard I tried to hide it. That shitty side of me would inevitably sell me out and she'd know from even the subtlest change in the tone of my voice.

But back to that alcohol-induced, split personally of mine.

The difference between Bryce and Bruce (yes, my wife named him) was downright frightening, especially to my wife and kids, who received the unpredictable brunt of Bruce's abuses (Bryce's too, who are we kidding?).

Even as I write this now, I cringe at who I was back then and the pain I caused the ones I love most. I am her husband and their father, for fuck's sake. God, I was a monster.

If you met me when I was sober, then you got Bryce Arnett: this sad excuse of a "man" who, despite his little-bitch victim mentality and overall loser ways, was still kind-hearted and somewhat tolerable. But if you happened to be around me when I was drinking (and/or hung around me long enough) then you got Bruce: that indelible bastard – manipulative, miserable, cold, cruel, and cunning, like a fucked-up fox. And while I'm definitely glad he's dead and gone, I'll always be grateful for him too.

If you've ever struggled with mental health (who hasn't) or you're struggling with it now (who isn't), then you know what it feels like to get bitch-slapped in the face with an identity crisis or two. And I'm not talking about your father's mid-life crisis, either. I'm talking about a legitimate *WTF* moment when a man looks himself in the eyes and out of fucking **nowhere,** he wonders just who the hell is looking back at him. That was me just a few short years ago.

It was the ignorance of myself that led to my split personality. After I got sober and started making some serious changes in my life, I realized that I didn't know who the hell I really was and I sure as shit didn't know who or what I'd become. All I knew was that I *hated* that man more than I've ever hated anyone in my life.

But guess what? I love that guy now. Why? Because without him, I wouldn't be able to serve and support men who've struggled with similar crises in their lives. Without him, I wouldn't be who I am today.

When you start rediscovering who you are, especially after *years* of self-harm, it can be a terrifying process for two reasons. One, you honestly don't have the first fucking clue who you are beneath the beast you've become, and two, what will everyone else think about the new/real you?

All I can say is that discovering who you really are – figuring out your passion and purpose in life and mending that split within you – is going to require time and obscene amounts of patience. I'm still working on it. We'll both be working on it for the rest of our lives. But we'll do it as a person with integrity, not as a spineless simp hiding behind a monster.

The Blame Game

You may succeed in making another feel guilty about something by blaming him, but you won't succeed in changing whatever it is about you that is making you unhappy.

–Wayne Dyer

It might seem easier to just blame everyone and everything for your fuckups in life. First of all, that bullshit is not only incredibly weak and as un-manly as it gets, but it also only serves to make matters worse for you the longer you continue to con yourself. So stop pointing fingers at everyone else.

When it comes to placing abject failures and miserable misgivings on others, I was a consummate pro. Sure, I've had people take advantage of me and my generous nature, but other than the occasional leech or parasite, it was pretty much just me fucking myself over. I was solely responsible for the consequences of my own actions. And that's a painful pill to swallow.

You give power to others over your life when you place blame on them for things that have happened to you. You also then give them power over your happiness, believing they can take it away at any moment.

I suppose that's yet another side-effect of being trapped in that victim mentality. You constantly tell yourself that things are too good to be true, that you don't deserve to be happy, or that you're unworthy of love, in general. And guess what happens when you tell yourself that shit? It comes to pass.

The key is to not only stop blaming others but to also not turn the blame on yourself. You can accept responsibility without the energy of blame. One of the hardest things to do when your mind is fucked up is to flip the script and start telling yourself that you are responsible for your own happiness and that you have the power to create it.

Changing and improving any area of your life is going to be uncomfortable. That is par for the course. Remember that you didn't get to where you are right now, overnight. It took time and patience to fuck your life up and it's going to take time and *more* patience than you knew you had to un-fuck it. But you must first start by accepting responsibility for it all and stop playing the blame game. The buck stops with you.

Embrace the Suck

Change is inevitable. Growth is optional.

—John C. Maxwell

So you're at the point where you know it's time to make some changes. Right on, brother. That's great. It's not easy to change your life for the better – if it was, everyone would do it. Discomfort comes with the territory. But brother, that is nothing compared to the pain of staying stuck for the rest of your life.

When it comes to the mental, emotional, and spiritual challenges you'll inevitably experience on the path to change, lean into that shit. Will it suck? Sure! *Embrace* the suck. Stop resisting change and go with the flow like you're cruising down an empty highway. Whatever you resist, persists. And if you resist the pain and discomfort that's required to change, then that's exactly what you'll continue to endure.

Listen, change isn't some simple, easy, overnight process. It's a lifelong journey – a one-way road riddled with speedbumps, potholes and idiot-assholes at every turn. But they're just distractions. And those distractions are designed to test your mettle, my man. They will manifest and appear in your life (and from virtually nowhere) in an attempt to veer you off course. That's not a matter of if but *when*.

Each time that happens is an opportunity for you to remain strong, stable, and steadfast. Stay consistent with the daily things you are doing to better yourself. And if anyone wants to play chicken with your awesome ass, then dare them all to bring it the fuck on. They'll either move aside, or they'll simply get run over. Stay the course.

Drop the Mic

You probably wouldn't worry about what people think of you if you could know how seldom they do.

—Olin Miller

This chapter may seem like a re-hash of the first one but being honest is perhaps the most important thing you will do on your road to a better future. It's downright terrifying to be open and honest with the world about what you've gone through or what you're going through right now. Trust me man, I know. Hell, it's tough enough just to be open and honest with yourself – since most men have no clue who they are in the first fucking place.

Men tend to hide, bury, or compartmentalize our shit. We attempt to pretend like everything's "A-ok" and act like we have it together when that couldn't be further from the truth. And instead of coping with our crappy situations constructively, we turn to pills, porn, drugs, alcohol and work to sedate the pain. We hold onto it instead of letting that shit go. And as a result, we have an epidemic of suicide on our hands.

Being open and honest about your checkered past or forthcoming with your current fuck-ups certainly is some scary shit to think about, let alone to actually act on. That kind of gesture takes courage. It takes moxie. It takes huge huevos. It takes a man. And how fortunate for you that you just so happen to possess all of those qualities in you right now.

When it comes getting shamelessly honest with the world – and especially when it comes to people you know, trust and love and those who know, trust and love you – the idea of sharing or owning your shit *can* (and should) freak you the fuck out. But so what? Brother, that just so happens to be one of the many good reasons why you *should* share your shit!

You're afraid they'll judge you? They will. Who cares! Those who won't support you can go, so be thankful while silently saying "sayonara". Then you move on and move the fuck forward.

You're worried what they'll think of you? Who gives a shit! At least you have the courage to be open and honest, and believe me brother, that takes balls. Big ones.

The best reason of all to share your shit is because when you do that (more often than not) it inspires others to share their shit as well. Moreover, it inspires people to forgive themselves and move forward with life. It gives them permission to accept themselves. And perhaps, somewhere down the line, because you shared, it might inspire someone you don't even know to completely turn his life around. And that's some noble shit right there and reason enough to get to sharing.

But the only way to find the courage to be honest is to grow a set, swallow your pride, deflate your ego, take a deep breath, and jump head-fucking-first off the cliff and into the beautiful unknown. Don't know how to fly just yet? Don't worry, son, because you have wings and you'll learn as you fall. You'll flap those fuckers fast enough. Trust me.

"But I'm a private person, Bryce." So was I, dude. Still am to some degree and always will be with certain things. But for the most part, I'm an open-fucking-book. Besides, I found out quickly just how supportive people are of you, especially random strangers or "friends" on social media.

Just don't post shit for attention or "likes", brother. Do it for **you**. After I did this, I realized not only how sweet and supportive everyone was but also that people are just plain forgetful. Society has a shorter attention span than a goldfish, and 99.99% of them are only thinking of themselves.

From my own experience, when you finally say "fuck it" and decide to share your shit, it'll be one of the most liberating, cathartic actions you'll ever take in your life. I encourage you to be transparent as fuck with people about your entire life, regardless of what you're going through.

Start small and tell someone you can trust. Maybe find a support group online or in real life – preferably real life, because human to human contact reigns supreme – then branch out from there. Because that's the only way to conquer fear, my friend, by doing shit that scares the fuck out of you.

Remember, your test is your testimony. Your mess is your message. Your shit is your… that one doesn't work. But you get the point.

You have a chance to start fresh. You have the opportunity to disarm your enemies by ripping from them any type of ammunition they think they have. Fuck 'em. Take that shit back. Disarm them completely.

Ever seen 8-Mile with Eminem? If not, at least give the end of it a watch. Do what he does at the end of that movie. He goes off and shares his shit. He lists off all the shit he's gone through and what he was going through then. He exposes himself by airing out his dirty laundry for all eyes and ears to see and hear.

And he owns that shit. All of it. And he does not give a single fuck what anyone thinks, including the stunned crowd standing in silence. At the end he tosses the microphone to his utterly defeated opponent and says, "Here, now tell these people something they don't know about me."

Free yourself from giving a damn about those who don't give a damn about you, brother. Bare your chest for all to see. Leave 'em speechless. Drop the mic.

Nobody Else's Life

Your biggest supporter is a stranger. Your biggest hater is someone you know.

—Heath Ledger

Negative people suck to be around. I should know, I *was* negative people, and I couldn't stand being around me. But you know the type I'm referring to, right? *Those* folks suck! *And* they suck the life out of you if you allow them to.

So let me impart some wisdom on you here in this chapter: You are not contractually bound to surround yourself with people who make you miserable. Period.

There's no nobility in sacrificing *your* wants, needs and desires, just to ensure someone else's are met. So stop it. Stop that shit right now. When you put someone else's needs above your own, you likely have low self-worth. Again, I should know.

I'm not talking about your children's or your family's needs here, either. As a parent, you have a moral and legal obligation to at least minimally care for the needs of your children. But the level of care you give them will match the level of care you give yourself. How can you truly take care of anyone else if you can't even take care of yourself?

You gotta fill *your* cup first. You can't rely on others to take care of you. You must do it for yourself. You must be the one to walk the path.

Soon after you've taken a few steps towards changing your life, you'll begin to notice who actually supports your growth, who champions that shit, and unfortunately, who resents it. And there will be those who resent it, rest assured. Not because they resent you, per se, but because your change highlights their lack of change. Your light reveals their darkness. Don't stop, though. Keep on shining that light no matter what.

To those making your life better, keep them around. Nourish and nurture those relationships. To those making your life worse, pluck them from the garden of life like the invasive weeds they are.

Start living your life for you and not for others. I'm not saying you should stop serving or supporting people. Not at all. Just be more discerning of where and to whom you give your time and attention. And don't ever lose sight of yourself in your desire to serve. If you do, one day you'll wake up and realize you don't know yourself.

They say that misery loves company, so if you're feeling miserable, then I'd say now is as good a time as any to take inventory of the company you keep, especially if that company is keeping you down. In other words, make the difficult decision to rid yourself of certain toxic relationships that aren't lifting you up.

People either make you smile, or they make you frown. Simple as that. If someone's dragging you down, drop 'em like it's hot. This is **your life!** Be it a friend, family member, or even your wife or girlfriend – some folks just gotta go. But hold up just a second. Because not *everyone* in your circle may be sucking your soul.

If you find yourself thinking "all of my relationships suck", well guess what, bud? The common denominator there is *you*. And if that's the case, then take some time to work on yourself first and then take inventory again. Then, if there are relationships in your life that still aren't supportive of your personal growth, they need to go.

You need to make room for relationships that have a positive impact and influence in your life. So look around you. Take note. Ask yourself this question, "Does my life suck balls?" If the answer is yes, then chances are that those inside your circle of influence suck balls as well. No offense, ball suckers.

I'm not saying it's going to be easy. I'm saying that in the long run, it's worth it. You can't continue to allow shitty people to clog your life. Flush them away like the festering, toxic turds they are. Then spray some air freshener to clear the funk and start working on yourself because you attracted those people into your life for one reason or another.

Set an intention that you'll meet new and exciting people who align with your true self – people who want you to succeed, people who will tell you the truth when it hurts the most; people who ground you, bring you back down to earth; people who tell you that you're fucking up and that if you're not careful, you're gonna lose it all.

And if you're making positive changes in your life and you notice that your friends and family aren't supportive of your growth? Set boundaries. Tell them you don't appreciate their pessimism. And if they still aren't supportive? My honest opinion? Forget 'em. Leave 'em all behind. You're better off focusing on yourself anyway.

When you begin to change your life, your energy changes too and there will always be people who are content with staying stuck or the same. But there's nothing you can do about that. So again, forget 'em. It's your life, not theirs. Live it accordingly.

Don't Worry Be Happy

Worrying is like a rocking chair: It gives you something to do, but it doesn't get you anywhere.

–Van Wilder

We suffer more often in imagination than in reality.

–Seneca

Kids are a perfect example of what it's like to live a proper, worry-free life. That's because they live in the moment. They have no real understanding of the past or the future.

They're not concerned with what they said to someone or anxious about tomorrow's deadline. They just focus on the present task at hand. They just are.

The next time you're around a young child who's just chilling on their own, take notice of just how incredibly present they are.

How "in-the-moment" that little one always seems to be. How bright and beaming their imaginations are before adults swoop in and shit on their shine.

How fearless they are before adults make them worried about shit they shouldn't be.

Little children don't worry about stuff like you and I do. In fact, they don't worry at all. They use their imaginations for fun and exciting things that seem impossible to adults.

Adults tend to use their imaginations to conjure up or dwell on the negative – the bullshit that doesn't even exist, except in their minds.

More often than not, when you worry about something, that something will manifest itself in your life. Good or bad, if you put energy out into the universe, the universe will return it in kind and possibly with amplified effect.

Worrying is essentially expecting the worst-case scenario. Whenever you expect the worst, you get it. But when you flip the script and expect the best possible outcome to a situation, what do you think the results might be then?

What if you throw worry away and replace that useless shit with a positive intention on how you want that outcome to resolve itself and then just let it go? Like when *you* were a kid full of pure potentiality, where anything and everything was possible, even if it was packaged inside your imagination?

Get back to being present like a child. If you can start to work towards that, then imagine the possibilities you can achieve as an adult. Stop suffering in your own mind. Accept the fact that your current reality is the direct result of your cumulative personality. It's the culmination of every choice you've ever made.

Own it and return to your innocence – a place where your imagination is still free to run as wild as you fucking want it to. You remember that little guy, don't you? Guess what? He's still in there. And he doesn't have a worry in the world.

Sharp Tongued Shithead

Words are, in my not so humble opinion, our most inexhaustible source of magic. Capable of both inflicting injury and remedying it.
—Albus Dumbledore

My tongue is wicked-sharp. Too sharp. Not as sharp as it used to be before I got sober, mind you, but it'll still slice and dice 'em like a samurai sword. If you have a sharp tongue like I do, then you must know what it's like to lose your cool and say shit you don't mean.

And if you have a sharp tongue, a short fuse, and you *are* or *were* a raging asshole of an alcoholic, then you definitely know what I'm talking about when it comes to saying crap you can't take back.

My wife, ever compassionate, patient and wise, used to tell me that she was glad I couldn't remember what I'd said to her when I was shit-faced drunk. She knew I already felt shitty for drinking and she didn't want me to feel worse.

God bless that woman's patience because when it comes to wielding words at someone, I am more than capable of slicing them to shreds with my tongue. It's not something to be proud of, obviously, and let's just say I've had to eat my own nasty words more times than I can count.

I've said some incredibly hurtful things. And I've said them to the closest people in my life. My wife and children, who took the brunt of my bullshit. My friends. My mom and dad. My brothers and sisters. Ex-girlfriends. Idiots on social media. But guess what? I don't do that anymore. I've learned it's a lot easier to think about what I'm about to say first, before I end up having to apologize for it later. Once something leaves your mouth, you cannot take it back.

When you begin to change your life, you have to start with changing your mind. More specifically, you have to think about your thoughts. And more specifically than that, you have to start paying attention to *how* you're speaking to yourself, in your mind. And that takes a **ton** of patience and a lot of practice. But that's how you get good at anything, right? And if you can control your thoughts, you can control the words coming out of your mouth.

Men should be wiser with their words; more cautious with what they say out loud and with the way they say it. This particularly applies to self-speak or self-think – how you converse with yourself, in your mind, if you will.

The conversations in your mind – the internal dialogues – are the ones you must master. The words you speak to yourself are the words you need to pay mind to, the language you need to place more positive focus and attention on.

Become ruthlessly committed to not just how you talk to others – which is important because you don't want to be a dick if you are one – but how you talk to *you*. And stop being so negative toward yourself.

Words are magic, my man. They're *so* powerful and important. They can be used to create worlds and to destroy them. They can unite the world or divide it. Wield them wisely.

Take a Breath

Between stimulus and response there is a space. In that space is our power to choose our response. In our response lies our growth and our freedom.

−Viktor Frankl

You might not be aware of this, but since boyhood us men have been brainwashed into buying the bullshit about how boys don't cry. We've been programmed to keep our emotions at bay. We've been conditioned to be emotionless, cold, hard, tough, stoic, and intrepid - to hold back our authenticity and stifle our full expression.

And as a result, we have millions of men walking about like ticking timebombs, ready to explode on unpredictable notice. Emotion is energy in motion. So what do we think is gonna happen when men are encouraged to force their emotions and feelings down? Ka-fucking-BOOM!!

That was me not long ago. A ticking timebomb prone to frequent and unpredictable emotional explosions. I was an ill-tempered man-boy for a very, very long time. The worst example being my tendency to road rage, where I'd lose my shit at the smallest slight.

Once I nearly ran a guy off the freeway just because he honked at me − all while my then-girlfriend, now-wife, sat terrified in the passenger seat next to me, screaming for me to stop, until the guy I was raging at could tell I wasn't backing off and promptly exited the freeway to escape me.

I've lost my shit on my wife and kids. Lost my cool on my mom and dad and my siblings, too. On my in-laws and even on my best friends… I've raged on them all. And I'd love to blame the booze for all my rage (and that certainly didn't help), but the truth is I was just a passive-aggressive pussy for most of my life.

I never learned how to communicate properly or direct my emotions constructively. I had to learn that shit on my own and learn it the hard way, through experience. Experience is a cruel teacher: it gives you the test first, and the lesson second.

What I've learned over the years and since I got sober is that between every thought and immediate deed there's a momentary pause wherein a world of infinite potential and possibility exists. And in that moment, you have a choice whether or not to act on that thought or to give it some thought before you act.

You never know what someone might do, and you never know what someone's going through in their lives or how they think and feel about something. So before you react through anger, hurt or frustration, take a deep fucking breath and consider your choices.

You're not always going to be able to control your emotions because, admittedly, some shit just enrages the fuck out of you. But you have a greater chance of controlling your actions if you just take a moment first. I beg of you, brother, take a pause and think about whether or not it's worth it, before you do something stupid.

You might hurt someone or someone might hurt you. And for what? Road rage? Some asshole at the grocery store? Some d-bag at the club? Because someone honked their horn? It's not worth it. But guess what? *You* are.

So the next time you feel like you're going to freak the fuck out, please pause for a moment, and take a breath, broheim. Get your head clear before you make a brash decision that might end up costing you greatly. You'll be glad you did.

Just Ask

I pray because I can't help myself. I pray because I'm helpless. I pray because the need flows out of me all the time, waking and sleeping. It doesn't change God. It changes me.

—C.S. Lewis

Don't allow your pride and ego to prevent you from asking for help or support, particularly if you're struggling with addiction, depression, or thoughts of suicide. Be humble enough to receive that help whenever it's offered. Because when you find yourself on the path of change (and no matter where you are on that journey), you're going to need a bit of help and even a few hand ups along the way.

That support may come from people close to you or people you barely know. Even if you think you're alone out there on the path – which for the most part you will be – I promise you that you're not really alone. There are plenty of people out there eager to help you, so long as you're willing to help yourself first. But don't wait for people to offer help, because you might be waiting a long time. You have to *ask* for that shit. And that can be scary.

Asking for help will mean you have to put away that useless pride men tend to carry with them like some false badge of honor. Once you've put away that pride, you not only ask for help, but you need to be in a state of mind where you can actually receive it as well.

Believe me, there is nothing wrong with receiving help. It doesn't mean you are less of a man. It doesn't make you weak. On the contrary, it takes a lot of strength to ask for help. And receiving help doesn't mean you're getting a handout. Because you don't need another handout, do you? Where's that gotten you?

Brother, when it comes to changing your life, what you want and desperately need is a hand *up*. And the more people see that you're actually committed to change, that you're doing the work, the more hands will appear, eagerly willing to lift you higher than Snoop D-O-Double-G!

But what about times when you're actually alone in the world? Maybe you don't have friends or family you can ask because you've fucked up majorly and everyone's bailed? Perhaps you're an orphan? What the fuck do you do then?

My suggestion is to pray. You pray your ass off, brother. Take a knee right now and pray to whom or whatever you believe in and you ask for help. Even if you have to plead for it and feel like a beggar because you're only doing it when you need something… you fucking do it.

It's simple. "Ask and ye shall receive. Knock and the door shall be opened unto you." But prayer alone won't get you the change you so desperately desire. God, Source, Zeus – whatever higher power is out there – can only help you if you are willing to receive the help you've been praying for.

Remember that nobody's coming to save you. You have to take action to help yourself. Everything you want and need to have a successful life, is there for the taking. But you gotta ask for it first. And you have to believe you deserve to receive it. Here is your first opportunity to just ask.

Cruel Intentions

You may fool the whole world down the pathway of years and get pats on your back as you pass, but your final reward will be heartache and tears if you've cheated the guy in the glass.
—Dale Wimbrow, The Guy in The Glass

At the end of the day, you're the only one who really knows your true intentions. No one else knows what's going on inside your head or heart, and no one knows what's going on when you're all alone in the dark and no one is watching.

But what if people could actually see your true intentions? What if people could have a peek inside your heart and mind and see if what rests inside is riddled with ill-intent or is pure in purpose and aim?

What about your wife, kid(s), or significant other? Your parents or siblings? Your friends and family? Your boss, coworkers, or employees? Business associates, or your congregation at church? Would you want *them* to see?

Imagine a world where everyone could suddenly see inside your mind. Does that make you feel uncomfortable? Make ya squirm a bit? Because it sure as shit makes me feel uneasy to think about that. To think about someone else being able to know my thoughts? Yikes. It's a good thing no one can, right?

Well, while nobody really knows your true intentions – not even those closest to you – *you* know them. *You* know the truth. And you can't run or hide from either the truth or from yourself. Eventually your actions will convey that truth and everyone will know it too. You're not fooling anyone, bro, least of all the guy in the glass.

Nowhere to Run

There's no shame in fear, my father told me. What matters is how we face it.

—George R.R. Martin

Everyone gets scared. Even the bravest men in history have been frightened little bitches before. It's what keeps men from doing things that might injure us, kill us, or both.

Fear is an inescapable part of life, but it sure as shit doesn't have to limit your potential or govern your choices on how you go about living. And the only way to conquer that crap is to follow in the footsteps of intrepid men who've gone before you. You get up in fear's face and scream, "Fuck you, Fear! I'm gonna do it anyway and I'm gonna do it my way!"

For so long, I lived a life void of self-love, being left to live from a place of fear. Any decision I made or thought about making felt foreign without it. It's what kept me clinging to both booze *and* my victim mindset, even though both were obviously killing me.

And in some fucked up fashion, fear felt familiar, comfortable. Life seemed empty without it. And as a result, a wall of fear formed around my heart that even love had a hard time penetrating.

Once I kicked the alcohol and put a hard stop on my self-suffering – not being a little bitch who blamed everyone and everything under the sun for my fucked-up life – I started to remember what it felt like to love myself again. Then, slowly but surely, I began deconstructing that wall of fear surrounding my heart, brick by brick.

As I began that process, it felt like coming out of a coma. Suddenly I'm pushing 40 years old and wondering not only where my life went, but also "what the hell had I been running from this whole time?" And when I was finally sober enough and of sound enough mind to accept the answer, it hit me like an upper cut from Mike Tyson. I had been running from myself, from the man I'd become and from the parts of myself I was too scared to discover.

That's when I made the difficult decision to face my fears and stop running from the mess I'd made of my life. In that moment, I made the choice, instead, to run straight at the storm, guns a blazing. Because when fate whispers to the warrior, "You can't handle the storm" the warrior whispers back, "I am the storm."

Brother, you can run from just about anything but no matter how hard you try, you can't outrun yourself. Trust me, I tried. But why would you want to, anyway? What is it about you that's so awful? What are you so afraid of?

The great lie perpetrating people, in general, is thinking that something outside of you has any power to heal or "fix" what feels fucked up within you. No amount of drugs, sex, booze, money, or running will fill that void.

First and foremost, stop digging a deeper hole. Put the shovel down and start ascending up and out of the hellhole *you* created. It's going to take a ton of strength and courage to stop running from your fears. But, honestly, the only antidote to fear is having the balls to face it and giving it a good ol' fashioned bitch-slap.

You have to have the courage to not give a damn what anyone else thinks. Most of the time people fear their imaginations more than they fear reality. Most of the shit you're afraid of is just "phantom fears" because they're all in your head – they don't exist elsewhere.

The law of the harvest applies perfectly to fear. You reap what you sow. If you sow fear, you will reap a life full of it. If you sow courage, well you get the idea. What are you so fucking afraid of that you're willing to choose a shitty life over living the one you were born to enjoy?

Whenever I get scared, I try to remember that it's probably all in my head and that fear is an acronym with two meanings: "Fuck Everything And Run" or "Face Everything And Rise".

My suggestion to you? Stop running and choose the latter to rise above what you're afraid of. Fuck fear.

Gratitude

Acknowledging the good you already have in your life is the foundation of all abundance.

–Eckhart Tolle

Because eking by in life wasn't the ticket for you, shit has to change. And that change begins and ends in the mind, brother. I **cannot** overstate that enough. As daunting as it may seem to work on one's mindset – like where the hell do I even *start* – one of the simplest, easiest ways to begin is by getting grateful for your life and every little thing in it.

What is gratitude? Gratitude is the gateway to having it all. My wife likes to say it's "drawing attention to that which *is* working in your life, rather than focusing your attention on what *isn't*." Make sense? In other words, what you think about daily is what will continue to manifest in your life. So if you constantly think about or focus on the negative aspects of life, life's gonna return that shit in kind.

On the flipside, the same goes for thinking about and focusing on the *positive* aspects of your life. And don't give me this, "What's there to be grateful for, Bryce?" bullshit. Please know that no matter how shitty life seems, there is *always* something to be grateful for. And I don't use the word always, often. Gratitude is enough to begin digging yourself out of even the deepest holes.

If it helps, think of gratitude as negativity's solvent. It's the antidote to anxiety. It dissolves those low-vibe emotions like anger, fear, regret, grief, and even sadness. Gratitude is a panacea for your heart and soul, and especially for the ailing mind.

The fastest and most effective way to shift your shitty attitude is to force yourself to think about anything and everything you're grateful for. It may only be a few, basic things to start – like something as simple as being grateful that you woke up today and that you have air in your lungs.

Keep it simple, start small, and soon enough you'll see that the more you practice gratitude, the more the list of what you're grateful for will grow. Say your list out loud too, if possible. It's more potent, I promise you. Do it first thing in the morning before your feet hit the floor. Try it in the car on the way home from work when you're super pissed or frustrated. It's pretty difficult to be grateful and angry at the same time.

Now go on and get grateful. And start by being grateful for you.

Tomorrow is Promised to No Man

Most people master the art of postponing the start.
                                    –Mokokoma Mokhonoana

Father Time. That old bastard's been battin' a thousand since the beginning of... time. He's perfect. And so is his scythe-slinging brother, Grim. Both are undefeated, have impeccable records, and are as consistent and unavoidable as the sunrise.

This is your reminder to have a healthy respect for both of those things – time and death – in terms of the finiteness of life itself and the inescapable reality that you never quite know when the Reaper will come wrapping at your door.

When I was a depressed and suicidal drunkard, I didn't fear the Reaper at all. I welcomed him. I was in a lot of pain, and when I stopped wasting my life away through drugs and alcohol and had to cope with that pain *without* the aid of drugs and alcohol to numb it, nearly three years passed before I finally felt even remotely "normal" again.

Once I started working on healing the underlying cause of that pain – ie my victim addiction – suddenly it dawned on me that I was nearly 40-fucking years old and had basically trashed the past 20 years of my life. That's when I grew sick and fucking tired of telling myself that "one day I'm gonna do this, that or the other."

I grew tired of underachieving. I grew tired of lying to myself. And it was time to make a change.

People put aside all the shit they really want to do because they think there's an infinite amount of time to do it "later." When is "later" exactly? I've wanted to write a book for most of my adult life and yet it's taken me this long to write one.

I don't know a whole lot and my ego is alright admitting as much. But brother, at some point there won't *be* another "one day" for me, or for you, or for any of us. There might not be another "one day" with the people you love and there might not be another "one day" for those people who love you. All of that and more can be taken from you in a flash. Everything in life is temporary and has an expiration date, including life itself.

So stop pretending like you have time to waste. Because to be brutally honest with you, brother, you don't. Stop saying "one day" and start living a "Day One" life. Tell yourself every morning that you're stoked to be alive, that you're grateful you woke up and have air in your lungs.

Don't let every day become like *Groundhog Day* because you don't have the courage to take a mitigated risk. That's what I did for years. It sucks balls, trust me. A "one day" life sucks. A "Day One" life is worth getting up for.

A Little Patience

God grant me the serenity to accept the things I cannot change, the courage to change the things I can, and the wisdom to know the difference.

–Reinhold Niebuhr

One of the hardest things for men to do these days is to practice patience and delayed gratification. Don't believe me? When's the last time you resisted the urge to make a "deposit" at the spank bank? Exactly.

For men, patience isn't just a virtue, it's a rite of passage. We live in an incredibly impatient and over-privileged society where everyone wants whatever-the-fuck they want, whenever-the-fuck they want it. Now we have *generations* of men who feel like they "deserve" something even though they didn't have to work for it or wait for it. And that ain't good.

Change is hard as fuck. It's going to require a shit-ton of patience. The path to change will present you with plenty of things hellbent on pissing you off, setting you back and slowing your roll. But the key is to remind yourself that you are more than worthy of having whatever it is you're longing for. You just have to be patient while you work for it.

I get that you might be an impatient man. I was one of the most impatient people ever. Just ask my wife. But now,

57

whenever I grow impatient, I remind myself that patience is a bitter plant, but it bears sweet fruit. Sometimes the worthwhile things in life only come to those who work patiently for them.

Try applying that technique to anything in life where patience or serenity is warranted: traffic, work, social media, politics, communicating with your significant other, chatting with your children or working towards a goal such as changing one or all aspects of your life.

Keep in mind that growth of any kind doesn't happen suddenly, either. You didn't get to where you are now overnight, did you? Change or evolution takes time. It comes through small, consistent actions that accumulate over weeks, months, and even *years* before one day, outta the blue, someone says to you, "There's something different about you."

That's when you know you've changed. That's an encouragement that will propel you forward and give you the self-confidence you need to keep going. So next time you feel like you just can't wait for [insert dream here], relax, take a deep breath, and reach for a little patience.

Forgive Your Father's Sins

To err is human, to forgive is divine.

–Alexander Pope

My dad was a dick, plain and simple. Not the worst one by any means, but he wasn't winning any "Father of the Year" awards. I haven't been the best dad either. I abandoned my boy and drank my daughters' childhoods away.

But I've long-since reconciled with my son and with my girls, and I've been sober since January of 2020. I've had the balls to admit my mistakes, ask my children to forgive me, and moved forward with life, unlike my dad.

He's dead now – passed away a few months before this book was born, but not before I began writing it – and when I was thinking about forgiveness and how much easier life gets when you learn to accept an apology you never got or may never get, my father always popped in my head. At the time our relationship was non-existent but I couldn't get him out of my mind.

So when he passed away and I had a few months to reflect on the complexities of our fucked-up excuse for a relationship, it dawned me that forgiveness and the father-son relationship are somewhat inseparable, at least in my case and perhaps most men's, as well. Perhaps even yours.

I cannot emphasize enough how my learning to forgive him for all the fucked-up things he did or said to me (and doing so face-to-face) was possibly the most significant and pivotal turning point for me in terms of healing my heart and mending my mind.

Even though the begrudging bastard couldn't acknowledge the errors of his ways at the time or muster a fucking apology for me or my siblings before his final breath, it didn't matter.

I forgave him for the way he treated me when I was 17, still in high school and got my girlfriend pregnant. I forgave him for calling me a serial sinner and never-ending disappointment; for calling my baby's mama a whore; and for calling my unborn son a bastard and abomination before the eyes of God.

I forgave him for not giving me an ounce of support or advice or wisdom of any kind, or even a smidgeon of fatherly guidance whatso-fucking-ever during my entire fucking life and specifically during the toughest time of my life, when I got my girlfriend pregnant.

None of that would've been a relationship deal-breaker on its own because getting her pregnant was *my* responsibility to handle, *my* mess to clean up. I get that shit, brother.

When I found out the breaking news that he'd fucked around on my mom back in 1981 and got *that* woman pregnant – all while my mom was pregnant with *me* – that's when our father-son relationship was shattered. I couldn't believe what a hypocrite he was. That's when he stopped being my dad and became my sperm donor instead.

I'll never forget getting the news, either. It was just one of those moments in life that a man never forgets. It was Father's Day 2001, and I'm doing my first stint in jail for attempted credit card fraud. I'd just finished talking to my son on a grimy payphone in Cell Block D when my mom jumped back on to say goodbye. She said she had some news and told me that I was gonna hear it anyway so I might as well hear it then.

She said a girl around my age showed up at the front door earlier that day and told whoever answered that she was my dad's daughter. Honestly, I don't remember the rest of the call other than feeling a sense of shock, confusion and sadness, followed by hardcore feelings of dismay, resentment and rage towards my unbelievably hypocritical father.

And those feelings towards my dad wouldn't go anywhere for a very long time. Not until ten years later when I finally learned to forgive him and let that shit go.

I remember sitting down with him and placing my hand on his knee, looking him in the eye and saying the things I'd always wanted to tell him.

First, I asked him to forgive me for any pain or hurt I'd caused him over the years – which I admit was a lot, since I wasn't the easiest son to raise. Second, I said to him that I forgave him for all the pain and hurt he'd caused *me*. Then I gave him a hug, got up, and I walked out the door. Short and sweet.

What was his response? Nothing. He didn't say a word. No "*It's okay Bryce, I forgive you too*" or even a "*Thank you for forgiving me, son.*" Nothing. Nada. And you know what? I couldn't have cared less. Still don't. I expected him to say nothing. Because I knew that's who he was, and at that stage, I didn't give a shit if he changed. And he never did.

His stubborn ass couldn't stop me from letting all of that go. I didn't need his blessing to forgive my father's sins. That was my choice, not his, and it was the most cathartic experience of my life. And when he finally passed a way over a decade later, it didn't hit me nearly as hard as it would have had I not been the bigger man. And I'm good with that.

So don't wait to make amends. Ask for or give forgiveness to your father, bro. Forgive. Forget if you can. Let go.

STFU & Listen

Most people do not listen with the intent to understand. They listen with the intent to reply.

–Stephen R. Covey

When was the last time you just shut the fuck up and listened to someone *without* waiting to respond with your own point of view? It's something we can all work on and it's vitally important to every person's growth when they feel like they're not only being heard but also being allowed to just fucking feel however they want to feel.

Men bottle shit up until we blow up on someone else or we blow ourselves away. That can't happen anymore. And I know there are times when it feels like no one's listening to a damn thing you're saying – that no one has the first fucking clue how you're feeling on the inside – but the best way to be heard is to learn how to hear others out first.

The reality is that the majority of people outside of your inner circle are too focused on their own problems to give energy to you and yours, nor are they really listening or paying attention to what you're saying. They're simply biting their tongue and waiting their turn to talk. And in all likelihood, you're just the same as they are. I was too.

Let me ask you this though: how often do you really listen to others?

Now by no means am I some world-class listener. I even had a t-shirt as a kid that read *"Help! I'm talking and I can't shut up."* I'm working at being a better listener because that's what the world needs more of right now: listening, understanding, compassion.

You can't expect someone to listen to what's going on with you if you won't listen to them. Kapeesh? Make sense? It should. If it doesn't, then go back and read it again and again until you get it. And this time, just shut the fuck up and listen.

Homies

Friends are God's apology for family.

–Tennessee Williams

Having a few solid friendships is a vital factor in every man's life, particularly if you came from a fucked-up family like mine. And although it might seem strange to be grateful that my family dynamic was dysfunctional (no offense, fam), I actually am just that – grateful. Because it made me see that even though I wasn't necessarily blessed with a fantastic family, it didn't matter because God was gonna bless me with a bunch of brothers from other mothers. Besides, who has a "normal" family anyway?

What is a good friend? A friend shares in your victories as well as your sorrows. A good friend tells it to you like it is. He won't hesitate to bitch-slap your overinflated ego and bring it back down to size. He has your back and is loyal to a fault. A good friend forgives you even if you inadvertently fuck him over. He teaches you things about yourself and is an impeccable reflection in terms of who you really are.

I've been fortunate to have some really great friendships in my life – friends who fit the bill when it comes to filling the gaps left vacant from that unfortunate family dynamic of mine. These friends exemplify what I personally believe it means to be a solid homie and confidant. And so this chapter is my acknowledgement and appreciation for those cherished friendships of mine; an homage or **bro**mage, if you will.

I have one buddy who taught me my unstoppable "rain or shine" work ethic. He wouldn't let me quit. He told me we were working no matter fucking what: wind, rain, sleet, snow or shine. I freaked out on this same friend one night, years later, when he tried calling me a cab so my wasted ass wouldn't drive. The next morning he sent me a text, making sure I got home okay. When I apologized for being a dick he said he didn't care about that. All he cared about was that his friend made it home alive.

I have a buddy I've known since we were four years young – my longest friendship and oldest pal. My junior year of high school I stole his truck and ran away with my girlfriend to Texas. He had every right to knock my teeth in for jacking his ride. When I was eventually pulled over and brought back home to Utah, he came over to my house and I fully expected him to punch me in the face. But he didn't. Instead of whooping my ass, he wrapped his arms around me and gave me a hug. Then he told me he was never worried about losing his truck – or pissed that I stole it from him – he was only worried that he wouldn't see his best friend ever again.

I have another buddy who I've also known for most of my life. He's the one whose mom's credit card information I stole when I was 20. She had known me for most of my life as well. Immediately after I was released from jail (for an unrelated offense) I called her to apologize and she actually forgave me – even mentioning how hard it must've been for me to call her. I called that friend right after I talked to his mom so I could apologize to him, too. He had every right to kick my teeth in (just like that other buddy of mine) yet didn't. He came over a few days later while I was under house arrest, with an ankle monitor strapped to my leg, just to tell me that he tried to hate me but couldn't.

There is also the friend who was nearly 30 years my senior, who despite my alcoholism and extreme self-loathing when we met, still saw the good in me and supported me like we'd known each other our whole lives.

And finally, there's the buddy of mine who called me one fateful morning to tell me that if I didn't stop drinking I was going to lose my wife and kids to my alcohol addiction. He lit into me and when I attempted to downplay the seriousness of my situation, he said *"This isn't fucking funny"*. He had to have really cared just to say what he said, because I know it wasn't easy for him.

I appreciate all of these men (and there are still more who I didn't mention here) for what they've shown me about myself and how they've helped me to become a better man. Hold on to the friendships in your life. The good ones. Sometimes they're the only family a man's got.

Good Fences

Whatever you are willing to put up with is exactly what you will get.
−Unknown

If it feels like you're surrounded by people who constantly take advantage of you, then it's time to take inventory of the company you keep. You desperately need to set some boundaries and make *your* needs non-negotiable. Otherwise, you're just a people-pleaser like I was. But if you're cool with that crap, then stop bitching about it, get used to giving until you're bone-dry, and plan on people walking all over you for the rest of your fucking life.

That was me for damn-near my whole life: a pushover and passive-aggressive asshole who resented all of his relationships because he had no boundaries. I was a prototypical people-pleaser and quintessential "yes man", and the more I found myself trying to please others, the less and less pleased I became with myself.

That was until I got sober, grew sick and tired of people taking advantage of me, and put a stop to that shit by building good fences and enforcing those boundaries if or when anyone ever crosses the line.

My man, if you want healthy relationships that support your upward aim, then rid yourself of the toxic ones holding you back or keeping you down. Know that you need to set some firm fucking boundaries when it comes to precisely what you'll tolerate and how long you'll tolerate it. Don't worry about offending other people's delicate sensibilities, either. Why should you, when it's obvious they couldn't care less about offending yours?

When you establish boundaries with someone – especially if there were none or very few before – they won't like it, and they will test them. That's because you didn't set any beforehand, so now that you've drawn a line in the sand, those people are gonna wonder what the fuck is going on. Keep in mind that setting boundaries means you actually care about the relationship and intend on saving it, not the other way around and if they can't cope, then it's adios.

If it seems like your friends and family aren't on board with your newfound desire to change, then consider the company you keep. Take a long, hard look at *every* relationship in your life – the good and the bad – and particularly the ones having the most impact on your life right now.

Then, if necessary – and believe me brother, it's not just necessary, it's crucial to your mindset and mental health – you have to rid yourself of those toxic people you're choosing to allow into your life. You know, the ones who essentially suck the lifeforce from you like a dementor. And as hard as that can and will be – and it *will* be – I assure you that it's worth it. Because guess what? *You* are worth it.

Contrary to popular belief, you are not obligated to surround yourself with people who refuse to treat you with respect or who make your life worse than it already is – you, yourself, have done a stellar job in that department already.

Seriously though, there is absolutely *no* nobility in setting yourself on fire just to keep the Deb & Donny Downers of the world warm. So break the cycle, brother. Those folks can find a new source of heat to keep them warm, figure out a way to make a fire, or they can fucking freeze. They are not your problem or concern any longer. Let them go.

No is a complete sentence. Get masterful at saying it. If it's not a fuck yes, it's a hell no, bro.

Out With the Old

Everything can be taken from a man but one thing: the last of the human freedoms – to choose one's attitude in any given set of circumstances, to choose one's own way.

–Viktor Frankel

Don't worry if your mind feels fucked up, imbalanced, or simply out of sorts, because brother you are free to change it at any given point. No one is stopping you. Nobody is keeping you caged. There's just you, dude. So what are you waiting for?

Oh, you're waiting on your circumstances to suddenly change. Ha! Good one. I used to tell myself that same bullshit story, too. Not gonna happen, though. You have to be the one to change. Only then will your circumstances change. So it's best to simply accept the aforementioned factoid as truth and begin systematically obliterating the old you by allowing the new you to move forward with fresh expectations. And having a good attitude is paramount to the process.

Look, I get it. Life isn't easy. And I know you know that. But what you may *not* know is that life isn't meant to be *this* fucking hard, either. And maybe what you (and men in general) need to hear is that the world isn't out to get you. God didn't curse or abandon you and who or whatever outside of you is not causing your grief within.

Life – as beautifully fucking brutal as it may be – is happening *for* you, not *to* you. More simplified, life is only as hard or as easy as you and you alone are making it. Don't believe me? Then riddle me this: of the vast number of variables in your life, which denominator is the most common and constant? It's you, pal.

That said, you also need to come to terms with the fact that it took a shitload of time, effort, sacrifice, and even some relatively impressive commitment to get yourself from where you originally started, to the personal *hell* you're in today. Therefore, I'd have you consider that it's going to require all of those things being maximized for your circumstances to "suddenly" change. Don't set yourself up for failure by believing otherwise.

Change is scary and downright terrifying at times. But so is the thought of staying stuck in your shitty ways, brother. Try not to focus on the fear and instead just focus on having a good attitude. Socrates said the secret of change is to focus all of your energy not on fighting the old, but on building the new. And the first good habit you'll start with is by thinking about your thoughts and getting control of your attitude.

You can't control what happens to you, but you sure as shit can control how you react and respond to it. Break the bad habit of talking shit on yourself, in your mind. Stop being so mean and cruel to yourself. And start telling yourself something positive, even if it feels fake at first. Fake it 'til you make it and you will…make it.

Humans are creatures of habit, and those habits dictate our daily lives. It's those little things we do subconsciously that we don't even realize we're doing until we suddenly have a shitty habit. That didn't happen overnight, it happened over time. And forming new, healthy habits works just the same. So be patient with yourself.

Because brother, you're a hard habit to break.

Comfort Kills Dreams

If your life ended right now, would you be happy?

–Ed Mylett

Your dreams aren't dead, dude. They're still plump and ripe for the plucking. It's just that you're figuratively or literally fat, lazy, and *way* too comfortable with where you're currently at. Plus you lack the proverbial balls to reach far, wide or high enough to grab those fuckers and put 'em in your front pocket. And I get that because I've been there before, so try not to pin your lack of achievements on your addictions, your family or your circumstances, like I did.

It's your mindset that's barricading you. And don't fret because I'm about to clue you in on a couple "dream hacks" I picked up when I thought my dreams – like this book – were dead and buried.

The first dream hack is that life happens outside of your comfort zone. What the hell does that even mean? It means life is all about expanding your capacity or capability to handle the extreme and unexpected. It means increasing your imagination and letting it run amok; pushing yourself past your perceived limitations; testing the outer limits of your "impossible" potential.

If you're willing to take the risk, then stepping outside your comfort level is going to require pushing yourself to the edge or extreme, all while making damn sure you don't venture too far beyond it. And next, I'll explain why.

The second dream hack dovetails off the first one, in that while you pretty much have to venture outside your comfort zone if you want to achieve the unachievable., what you *do not* want to do is go so far beyond it that you hit your "shock zone" or extreme "WTF is going on" mode.

If you get zapped out there, you're likely to contract again, which means going back to your previous comfort level. And not only are you running the risk of getting chucked back to where you started, you run the risk of regressing even further back than before. That's like taking 2 steps forward then flinging yourself 10 steps back. And that's just counterproductive to the whole fucking point, right?

Before I stopped drinking and even after months of being sober, my life used to feel so confined and contained. My dreams? What dreams? Fuck 'em, I was content inside my comfort bubble. I was used to it. Only it wasn't comfy or cozy at all, actually. In reality, it was super uncomfortable all the time. I got *so* used to feeling like shit that feeling shitty felt comfortable. Any time I started to feel better, I just missed the shitty discomfort of my bubble and would go right back.

There would be moments of clarity where I realized how far behind the game of life I was. Suddenly this surge of energy would hit and I'd try to make up for lost time by loading more shit on top of an already overloaded and overflowing platter. And when that happened, it meant I had sprinted past my comfort zone and I'd get snapped back like a rubber band when I realized I'd reached my shock zone. Make sense?

We live in a time when it's never been easier to completely reinvent yourself and become the badass you were born to be. But you have to be willing to go to certain extremes within yourself in order to get there. Extremity expands capacity but your shock zone will zap you right back. So just keep that in mind.

It's going to be rough. It's going to get uncomfortable. And the more you begin to push past the limits of what you once perceived was possible, it's going to get even **more** uncomfortable. It's gonna suck. And when it does, lean into it. Embrace the opportunity to grow.

Get comfortable being uncomfortable, brother, and God will make sure you're comforted along the way.

You Are What You Think

As a man thinketh in his heart, so is he. A man is literally what he thinks, his character being the complete sum of all his thoughts.
—James Allen, As a Man Thinketh

If you want to change your life – be that your body, your relationships, your money situation, your connection with a higher power, or anything else – *you are bound <u>only</u> by the limitations of your mind or imagination*. Period. End of story.

I suspect some men out there will disagree with me here that the mind is the stem, the genesis, the singular point from which all of a man's problems (and conversely his solutions) begin. And they're entitled to their opinion and perspective. But I wonder how many of those men have ever changed an unsavory aspect of their lives using only the power of the mind.

You can't always choose or change your circumstances or situation – as shitty as those may be – but you better bet your ass when I say that you can *always* control your thoughts and choose your attitude. You have commanding authority and absolute autonomy there, pal. And unless you're under some form of mind control, you're behind the wheel and no one else.

You own those six inches of invaluable real estate between your ears. That asset is *yours*. No one else can claim that shit but you. And as cliché and lame as it may sound, changing my mind changed my life.

The first place I started was by becoming ruthlessly committed to my thoughts and how I was talking to myself in my head. Once you begin to consciously track your thoughts and self-speak – and I can't understate how challenging this process truly is or how **vitally** important this is to changing your life – you'll start to catch yourself thinking like a whiny little bitch.

You catch yourself because you'll notice that those thoughts sound like how someone trapped in the victim mindset would speak. Then, over time, you'll begin to have "better" thoughts that sound more like a motherfucking warrior's than some weakling's.

That's when you know you're on the right path. Noticing you have a problem is the first step to changing it. Keep listening to yourself, course correct when needed, and as you do, your self-talk will change and become more supportive of the new you.

A better life begins with building better thought patterns. If you don't change them, then nothing changes and you'll stay stuck because you are what you think before you are anything else.

Balancing Act

Next to love, balance is the most important thing.

–John Wooden

The vast majority of men tend to focus all their time and energy on only one aspect of their lives – mainly money, since that's what most men mistakenly tether their self-worth to – while leaving the other more "important" stuff like love, joy, and true fulfillment, to wither and die.

But what about your physical health? Your relationship with those close to you? Your connection to God or to your spiritual side? Don't those areas deserve some TLC too? The answer is obviously yes, but the bigger question is: how do you manage to dedicate time or "balance" all of those individual (yet majorly time-consuming) aspects of your life? With something called Core 4, my friend.

Core 4 simplifies the balancing act process by breaking your life down into more manageable groups: your body, your spiritual connection, your family or personal relationships, and last but not least, your fun tickets or finances.

From there, it's far easier and more manageable to take a bird's eye view and see where you need to delegate more time and attention or what areas need a bit more balance.

You're never going to be able to carve your time up into equal pieces and dish them out evenly among all the people, places and things in your life. But what you can do is bring attention to each of those areas, so nothing gets forgotten.

The idea behind Core 4 is to schedule *some* time every day to each of those things and ruthlessly commit yourself to sticking to the schedule. That's it. That's how you juggle all the balls. That's how you find balance in life. You fucking *create* it.

Life is a balancing act and achieving perfect, static balance in life is bullshit. It's not possible. It's a fairytale myth. And buying into that bullshit story of "perfect balance" is a recipe for failure, not success. And you stopped believing in bullshit stories a long time ago, didn't you brother?

Higher Love

My trust in a higher power that wants me to survive and have love in my life, is what keeps me moving forward.

–Kenny Loggins

My faith in God began diminishing long before I started drinking. The addiction just shut it off completely. Organized religion – coupled with a hypocritically pious father who rarely, if ever, practiced what he preached – sort of soured me to the whole notion of God.

Fortunately for me, my faith in a higher power has been restored. Brother, let me ask you this: Do you believe in a higher power? Do you believe in God/Source/Creator? If you don't, then you may not believe me when I tell you that you have that higher power within you. Or that in a subtle, yet profound sense, you yourself are an extension of God. You wouldn't believe me then, would you? Or *would* you?

Okay, I'm getting way ahead of myself. Let me start over. Do you believe in God? And not necessarily "the God" commonly portrayed as a bearded old white guy, sitting high upon his gilded throne, groaning at the never-ending stream of freshly dead souls wondering, with bated breath, whether God's gonna to give 'em a high five and the greenlight to mosey through the Pearly Gates of Heaven, or shake his crowned head, give 'em the thumbs down and damn their sorry asses to an eternity of Hell. Nah, I'm not talking about *that* God.

What about *any* God? Source? Spirit? The Universe?

It's okay if you don't. I didn't. Not for a long time, at least. But I did when I was a boy raised in a Christian-based religion. And I can vividly remember how I would spend hours lying awake at night and pondering those "unanswerable questions" of life like: *Is there a God; Where did I come from; Does space go on forever; Is there life after death; and What's the deal with dinosaurs?*

And honestly, I can't recall when it was but at some juncture, I just lost touch with God and my spiritual side. I stopped believing in a "higher power" altogether.

However, I do vividly recall those nights when I was so hammered and felt so fucking worthless that before I passed out, I would pray hard and beg God to take me from this earth, to ease my pain and end my existence. I'd beg him to take me in my sleep. Then when I'd wake up in the morning with a hangover, I'd curse him for not answering my prayer, supremely disappointed I hadn't died.

Once I got sober, that part of me that believed in a higher power slowly began to reemerge, not that it takes one to have the other. I began noticing the synchronistic things in my life and opened myself up to the idea that there are spiritual beings which actually want to help us with our problems.

Now, I'm not going to get all preachy and tell you what to believe in. Beliefs are incredibly sacred and personal things. But I'd have you consider that you are living proof there's a higher power.

And if you've attempted suicide and survived – or survived **anything** that by all measures you probably "shouldn't have" – then how much more proof do you need that there exists a higher source of power than yourself? Perhaps there is a reason that you are still here.

Factor together all the crazy shit that had to happen just for you and me to be born – like our parents meeting (and boning), their parents meeting (and boning), and so on and so forth – the odds are something like 1 in 400 *quadrillion* (yes with a Q) that we became us. Those are some God-level odds, brother.

All I'm saying is that at this stage of the game, in terms of the absolute evil wanting to take over the world, I personally believe you need to believe in something – anything – that helps you understand that you actually have something you can tap into when all hope seems lost.

In a Blink

You can fail at what you don't want, so you might as well take a chance on doing what you love.

—Jim Carrey

Twenty years from now you will be more disappointed by the things you didn't do than by the ones you did do.

—Mark Twain

If there's anything I've learned from those decades I spent misusing my temporary time here on Earth, it's this: life is incredibly fucking short, second chances are few and far between (so don't fuck them up) and if you wait to do the shit you want to do and always dreamed of doing, before you know it... you'll have run out of time.

And I know you'd rather be spending your final days reflecting on all the cool things you did and all the rad people you did them with, rather than lying on your death bed spending your final moments wracked with regret for not doing the things you wish you had.

I missed a large portion of my son's life because I was a deadbeat dad and simply bailed on him. Can't blame the booze for that one. And I missed a good chunk of my girls' lives as well when I was a miserable mess who drank away those precious moments that are gone for good.

I'm proud of myself for kicking the alcohol and getting sober so I wouldn't miss more memories with my children. I'm grateful for the son I abandoned, who has chosen to allow me to rekindle our relationship once again. And I'm thankful that my girls don't remember their drunk monster of a dad. Nevertheless, I'm human and I'm still healing, and sometimes it's hard not to feel like a complete and total POS for drinking all those memories and possible memories away. But waddya do?

You'll never get back time, obviously. But the one thing you can do is use the time you have now wisely, from this point forward and make the most of it. The last thing you want is to look back on life and wonder *"What if?"*

And I know it's hard to not get caught up in the past, but, brother, it's time to let go. And I'm writing this part for me, as well, as a reminder that whatever it is you're dealing with, it's temporary. You just gotta believe me. Everything is temporary, including life itself.

Take chances. Chase your dreams at all costs, regardless of if the odds are stacked against you.

Stop living in the past and enjoy the present so that you can ensure your future fucking rocks. And never forget what William Wallace says in the movie *Braveheart*, "Every man dies. But not every man truly lives."

The Askhole

Give advice; if people don't listen, let adversity teach them.
—Ethiopian Proverb

At some point you might encounter the ever-so-frustrating and all-too-annoying Askhole. I should know, I used to live with one... me. And since I *was* one, I'm kind of an authority on askholes when it comes to how you deal with them and how you stop being one yourself.

You might be wondering what exactly an "Askhole" is? You know the type. That dude who constantly asks for the same advice or opinion yet rarely, if ever, fucking takes it. Then he has the gall to lie and pretend like he took it, while claiming it didn't work and was crap advice to begin with.

It's the guy who is always asking for favors but rarely offers anything in return. Sound familiar? Does that sound like anyone you know? Are *you* the askhole, perhaps?

I'm gonna give you the benefit of the doubt and assume you're not an askhole. So then, what might an askhole do if he wants to stop being one? You know, for "educational purposes"?

First and foremost, stop doing what I mentioned above. Stop asking and start heeding. If you really want someone's advice, then take it. Don't just ask so it seems like you're looking to change, when really you have no intention of doing the work it takes to change. If you frequently ask for favors, think about ways (not necessarily involving money) that you can reciprocate those favors.

If you personally know some askholes – acquaintances, associates, family, friends, employees, coworkers – whether you like it or not, they're a somewhat inescapable part of your life.

So set some boundaries. Either call them out on their bullshit or simply say *no* when they ask for advice, your opinion or a favor. Save your time, energy and resources for the ones who actually take advice and opinions and those who truly appreciate your help.

Brain Dump

Write hard and clear about what hurts.

–Ernest Hemingway

At some point during their day, I think most men typically have the overwhelming urge to sit upon their porcelain throne and drop a black pickle in the toilet bowl below. For some of us, we can set a watch to it. It's almost routine.

But what might happen if you applied a version of that routine to the mind and, like your belly, you crapped out all those shitty thoughts onto a sheet of paper, and removed or flushed them from your mind?

Like your bowels, your brain is also susceptible to constipation, in need of some sweet release. I know you know the feeling. Not the sphincter stretching kind, but that skull-stretching kind – that pressure building in your brain, ready to explode at a moment's notice.

Or better yet, your brain is a pressure cooker. And what do you think happens if that pressure valve fails to release all that skin-scalding steam? BOOM!! That's the way you have to look at your brain, like it's a pressure cooker searching for sweet release.

That was my mind for most of my life – a pressure cooker with no release valve – a colon full of crap and no toilet bowl below for me to empty my bowels into. It was common for me to just explode, for no reason at all, and anyone within the blast radius was sure to get plastered with shit.

But since I always liked to write, I figured that maybe I could just unleash that crap onto a piece of paper, instead of on my poor wife and kids. So I gave it the old college try and guess what? It worked.

My man, something's gotta give and it's gonna give somewhere in your life. And I know you don't want your anger and frustration to erupt like a volcano and spew molten hot lava all over the people you proclaim to love most, but without any other means of sweet release, it surely will. That's why you have to create that for yourself.

So at any point during your day if you're feeling the urge to purge (morning, noon, and/or night), feel free to take a "Brain Dump." It's sort of like journaling, except it's not. Similarly, though, you'll release all of your crappy thoughts onto a sheet of paper. And here's how you do it.

1. Don't worry about having congruent thoughts. None of it needs to make sense at all, whatsoever. You're stuck in your head too much as it is. No one's gonna read it, so… fuck it.

2. Write the first things that come to mind, get those out of the way, then repeat the process until the "toilet paper" wipes clean.

3. Toss that shit in the trash. Or, better yet, burn that shit. Watch it go up in flames and smoke and vanish.

4. Repeat the process until your brain – like your bowels – feels lighter.

Again, it doesn't need to make sense at all. Just grab something to write with and anything to write on and release the pressure cooker of your mind so it doesn't explode on others. No one likes to be covered in someone else's shit.

Quiet Please

Silence is true wisdom's best reply.

—Euripides

Did you know that the typical person averages between 6,000 to 75,000 thoughts per day? I say those are rookie numbers needing some pumping up, because most days it feels like *my* thoughts average around the million-a-day range. And for the longest time – especially during all those years of depression, anxiety and addiction – the only solution I could think of to quiet the onslaught of thoughts, was to put a bullet in my brain.

It's clear that I chose a less permanent solution to the temporary problems causing chaos in my mind. But how? These days, whenever my mind feels like the Energizer Bunny on Redbull spiked with an 8-ball of cocaine, it's imperative for me to find a space somewhere, any-fucking-where, in which I can allow my brain time to rest, relax, and simply shut the fuck up – to be present, if you will. Some call that meditation, but I call it... well, meditation too I guess, since I can't think of a better word.

Nevertheless, if you're like me and it feels like your mind runs nonstop, then you also know what it feels like when you want to run to the garage, grab an awl from the toolbox and drive that fucker deep in your dome just to get some peace and fucking quiet for a change. If that's you, then you need to give your brain a break, brother.

You need some form of mediation. Meditation can be incredibly challenging when you're just starting out. That's why we, as men, **must** create time throughout the day to put our minds in a much-needed timeout.

To me, that simply means doing something where I'm able to cancel out the white noise in my mind, make my immediate surroundings disappear and be as present as humanly fucking possible.

When I was a teenager I would shoot hoops for hours every day. I love to play basketball. It's my happy place and when I do it I am super present and my mind is empty. Now I workout for that quiet time.

Just find that thing you love to do and do alone, something that requires you to be present. That could be reading, walking, taking a shower, sitting quietly on the shitter, hiking, shooting hoops, firing off guns, or camping in the mountains with a fat cup of mushroom tea.

Whatever it is that allows you to be present, where nothing else really matters except for what you're doing in that moment, do more of that. And we'll just call whatever that is "meditation".

The Rising Tide

The noblest art is that of making others happy.

–PT Barnum

Like many men before me, I was really good at tearing others down. Too good, in fact. Which isn't good at all. It's not good to manipulate people's feelings and emotions or mess with their hearts and minds. That type of behavior is just plain fucked up – the type reserved for sociopaths and politicians – not good, honest men such as you and I. And we *are* good men, brother. If we weren't, I wouldn't have written this book and you wouldn't be reading it.

It's also an influenced or learned behavior, meaning you weren't born to rip others down; you were born to lift them up. And now, more than ever, men are being ripped to fucking pieces by too many everyday-life factors for me to list here. Men are meant to create and unite, and I am going to suggest something that fosters *that* type of behavior, not its polar opposite.

Since you're in the process of changing your life, why don't you consider lending a hand to another brother out there who's looking to change his as well? Because if your tide can rise, then that means others' can rise too.

When I made the conscious decision to stop exhibiting behavior where I essentially used people for my own personal gain, I thought about how I could flip the manipulative script and maximize my "talents" to raise people up, instead of raze them to the ground, to lift their spirts instead of crushing them. That's who I *really* am and that's what really brings me joy: serving and supporting people, particularly men, because, well, I am one.

When you're able to offer someone a hand up, and they actually take it, further on in life that person is far more inclined to pay it forward. Imagine a world where instead of there being such a cutthroat, competitive nature among men, there is this collective sense of cooperation and camaraderie?

We're warriors, not weenies. And often times I wonder what would happen if we utilized that warrior spirit within and actually used our competitive nature not just to protect our finances from going bankrupt, but to protect our basic morals and values from becoming bankrupt too; to use our innate competitiveness to drive growth in the hearts of men instead of stabbing them in the back.

While there's undeniable strength and power in the collective, the source of that strength and power comes from the individual who holds conviction in his heart for something good in the world that's worth fighting for.

A man named Alfie Kohn wrote a book called *No Contest: The Case Against Competition.* Mr. Kohn spent over five years researching competition for his book (and has the reference section to prove it) and what he discovered was that his initial hypothesis was wrong. Before he began his research, he felt that competition was detrimental to our psyche but that it was necessary to advance society. The more he researched, he realized that not only was competition more damaging than he originally theorized, it also was *not* necessary to advance society. Innovation is actually increased *more* through collaboration, *not* competition.

Remember, it's easy to tear someone down, especially when you feel low. After all, misery just *loves* company. But it's a lot more rewarding to lift others up. And the more you help those around you, the more you will be lifted by those who can help *you*.

So brother, if you have strength left in you yet, then you have what it takes to offer a hand up. All you gotta do is extend your arm and grab a hand in need. They're out there. Find them.

A Helping Hand

The best way to find yourself is to lose yourself in the service of others.

–Mahatma Gandhi

Listen my man, I want to be sensitive to your plights but I also can't pussyfoot around any of these topics. In this chapter, I'm not going to talk about my personal bullshit. Because from personal experience, I know that it really fucking sucks when someone tries to compare their bullshit to yours in a vain attempt to make you feel better about your bullshit. And I hope you haven't gotten that vibe from me in this book. I've eaten enough humble pie in my life to give Joey Chestnut a run for his hotdog inhaling money.

This chapter isn't meant to minimize or diminish your problems but sometimes it's good to be reminded that right now, someone, somewhere, somehow, is worse off than you are. Because when I stop and think about it, even at my worst, I still had it pretty fucking good.

Sure, I've been in and out of jail, experienced a brief bout of homelessness, dealt with depression, addiction and suicide, and I've been broke as fuck more times than I can count. But that shit is relative, right? All in all, life's been fairly fair to me. And I'll bet if you thought about it, you'd see that life's been fairly fair to you as well.

I believe that if you're still on the sunny side of the dirt, then there's still a fighting fucking chance for you to change your life. Don't take that for granted. As long as there's air in your lungs, there's work left to be done and life left to be lived.

Assuming it's not your first rodeo with mental health or addiction issues, a great way to help yourself through tough times is to hold on to the fact that you've been through hell and back before, danced with the devil and managed to survive at least one - if not many - personal dumpster fires. That means you have experience in those areas. That means you have real-life knowledge to share. And that means you can serve and support others who might *also* be going through hell right now.

I tell you this from personal experience: there isn't a drug I've tried or drink I've drunk that gets me higher than helping someone out by volunteering my *time*. Because that's the one thing you can't put a price on, since you can't buy more of it.

And I don't care what anyone says, time is the most invaluable currency in the world. When you give someone your time and dedicate a slice of it freely and without expectation, it's like you're donating a small part of your life to them. My point is that giving money is cool but giving your actual fucking time is the equivalent of a generosity trump card. You can't top time.

I don't care who it is or what it's for so long as it's a positive endeavor. It's science. I think? So if you've ever been down but managed to bounce back up, help another brother do the same. Show him how. Offer a hand-up, not a hand-out. One of the ways I've been able to help myself is by offering others a hand-up when I can. Simple as that.

That's how I got sober. Because another brother decided to tell me I was fucking up my life, and that I was about to lose my family if I didn't wake up. Another brother after that offered me support for the first 30 days of my recovery phase. Both of them helped me and if they hadn't, I wouldn't be here to help you. This, my good man, is the way.

I personally haven't found or seen a more beautiful method to understanding an people other than just shutting up and listening to their gripes – legitimate or not – and just being in service of others when they legitimately need (and want) help.

That's why whenever people ask me what I'm good at or what I enjoy doing, my answer to both is: people. Then, I clarify my answer by saying that the only person I actually enjoy doing is my wife. Haha. Everyone else I just enjoy helping. I love making people happy-er. That shit gives me a high like no other. No substance on earth can touch that rush. Trust me.

Now *you* give it a try.

Don't Be a Dick

No act of kindness, no matter how small, is ever wasted.

–Aesop

Contrary to what we've been led to believe, men have a buffet of constructive outlets through which we can vent our thoughts, feelings and emotions; so many ways we can blow off steam. However, we're sort of told the opposite when we're boys: to choke down our emotions, bury them deep and no matter fucking what, you better not cry or someone's gonna give you something to fucking cry about.

We're told that having emotions makes men weak, soft, and vulnerable. Like a girl. In less words, you're a pussy if you exhibit any sort of emotion. Sound familiar? It does to me.

In reality, holding all that in just makes you angry. It makes you mean. It turns you into a dick. And trust me, nobody likes an angry dick.

I mention emotions a lot in this book (in case you haven't noticed), and that's because *not* dealing with them is (one of) men's biggest problem(s). But is showing your emotions really weak, soft and un-manly? That bullshit could not be further from the truth, brother.

Contrary to that historical failure of a fable I mentioned above, I believe that if you *can't* express or get in touch with your emotions, then you're probably the one who's weak. Maybe *you're* the pussy. But since you're here, I think it's safe to assume you are not. Even if you are, then you're still in the right spot, because you need to read this shit.

Brother, a calm man is not a weak man. And don't confuse a man's kindness for weakness, either. That's a mistake. A kind man is a strong one because it takes strength and restraint these days to be kind and not be a dick and not kick some wannabe (keyboard) warrior's ass.

A calm man is an incredibly dangerous man who's learned to keep his cool. He's a Ford pickup from the 1990's – "like a rock". He's a lighthouse that's constantly being battered by punishing waves from a brutal storm, serving as a beacon of light for those sailors caught out in it. And you know that when the storm passes, he'll still be there. Waiting. Ready. Prepared.

Another important thing I feel compelled to add – since I know tons of men have a hard time controlling their tempers, including yours truly – is if you encounter someone who seems to be a few cards short of a full deck, please be aware of a few things.

One, you never know what someone is going through, so sometimes it's better to just walk the fuck away. Two, you never know who's strapped or carrying a firearm these days, brother, so sometimes it's better to just walk the fuck away. And finally, you never pick a fight with a guy who has cauliflower ear, so sometimes it's better to just walk the fuck away.

One of the hardest things to do is remain cool, calm and collected when you're on fire and seeing red. And some situations call for that type of behavior. But most don't. There's such a divisive narrative being pushed these days and it's being pushed on purpose. Don't buy into it.

Listen to your inner-calm, that stoic inside of you that knows he's a dangerous man who has his emotions under control. And regardless of what anyone thinks, these words have helped me during those times I've wanted to rip a man's eyes out and skull-fuck him: just walk away or kill him with kindness instead.

Leaders Are Readers

The more that you read, the more things you will know. The more that you learn, the more places you'll go.

–Dr. Seuss

When it comes to the multitude of factors that helped me change my life – the pivotal things that took me from a down and out fucktard drunk to a sober advocate of men's mental health – inundating myself with as much positive crap as humanly possible was paramount.

For the first 30 days of my sobriety, I completely cut out everything having a negative impact on my life. That meant putting a hard-stop to all social media, all TV (including sports and *especially* the news), all low-vibe music, any movies that weren't comedies or family movies, and anything on the world wide web that was sucking my soul dry. Particularly "ahem" porn. And once I eliminated most of the negative shit, my attention and focus turned to all the positive stuff I'd been avoiding for the past umpteen years.

I began exclusively consuming positive content like my life depended on it. Because frankly, it did. I read and watched anything and everything uplifting, inspiring and motivational. I pounded podcasts, devoured books, and occasionally watched movies that made me laugh – like RomComs (don't judge me).

Reading the right stuff matters too, so make sure it's something that's providing positive growth to your life. I grew up in a time when Reading Rainbow was appointment television... in *school*. That show was dope. Just thought I'd pay tribute to it. One of the only ways to expand your mind and recapture your impossible imagination is through books. So remember, reading is FUNdamental.

What helped me most during those first 30-days was reading all about the mind, since that's from where I personally believed all my craziness stemmed. That's when two books crossed my path – books I recommend to any man I know or come across who's struggling with the same or similar shit as I was. And they're the only two books I recommend in this entire book. That's because they genuinely had the greatest impact on my life and because they helped me fucking save it.

These two books are: *As a Man Thinketh* by James Allen and *You Are the Placebo* by Dr. Joe Dispenza. *As A Man Thinketh* is essentially about how we create everything in our reality through the mind. For those of you not already familiar with Dr. Joe Dispenza – he rebuilt his crushed spine in 9 weeks using only his mind. If you haven't read these books yet, do it. If you have, great.

These books were **the most** instrumental factors for my personal journey when I was at the end stages of feeling like absolute dog shit and at the beginning stages of wanting more from life. Read 'em. Don't read 'em. That's up to you. But if you do, they will provide you with the foundational and inarguable truth that we are 100% responsible for our minds and, by extension, our lives.

And if it helps, someone out there has gone through exactly the same shit as you. That person wrote a book about it and how he/she managed to rise above it. They turned their failure into a success, and success leaves clues. Follow in their path.

Most men's minds are locked right now and they sit miserable behind bars in a prison of their own making. Books are the key to opening that lock. Books are the key to freeing your fucking mind. So read them. All of them.

Buy all the books and read ten at a time and only a chapter per book. Have some fucking fun with it like when you used to actually enjoy reading. And if you don't have the time to read, then get the audiobooks. There really is no excuse. If you ever plan on leading, plan on lots of reading.

Growing Pains

There is no normal life free of pain. It is the very wrestling with our problems that can be the impetus for growth.

—Fred Rogers

Your new life will cost you your old one, bud. That's the brutal fact and painstaking prerequisite that comes with altering any aspect of your life that isn't serving you well. It means making room for a fresh start by killing whoever the fuck it is you've allowed yourself to become. And that means enduring even *more* pain than you've endured so far.

Pain means you're ready for change and change comes when the pain of your current lot in life outweighs the fear of changing it. You've had enough of your own shit, so to speak, and you don't know exactly how but you're ready to discover or rediscover who you really are. Who you were: before the depression; before the addiction; before the fucked-up thoughts and feelings and uncontrollable emotions; before the unimaginable pain, guilt and grief; before your past began to haunt your present; and most importantly, before the world dimmed down your motherfucking shine.

You're going to see shitty times. You're going to encounter plenty of dickheads along the way. And you're going to get fucked. Take your licks and keep on tickin'. Stop the needless suffering. You've already suffered enough, brother.

So continue along the path of change, even if it's painful as hell. Understand that there are many growing pains along the path of healing and self-discovery. They're temporary. You'll cope.

Pain is a good thing. Sometimes the best of things. Because if nothing else, it lets you know you're still alive. Take that pain, be it physical, mental, spiritual, emotional, or all of the above, and use it to grow and evolve as a man. Toughen your skin. Don't run from it either, use that shit to your advantage.

Pain is an inevitable part of life. Suffering is a choice. The difference between the two is as simple as choosing between remaining a perpetual victim or using that fucked up experience to propel you towards a victor mindset – the mindset of a fucking warrior.

No More Excuses

If you really want to do something, you'll find a way. If you don't, you'll find an excuse.

—Jim Rohn

My man, I don't know you nor do I have the first fucking clue who the hell you are, where you've been, how far you've come, or any idea what you're actually capable of in your life. I don't know your "story" from Adam's.

But I've heard enough men talk about their stories and you know what? They're pretty much all the same: total bullshit. And the moral of the story is often the same: men blaming anyone and everyone except themselves for the shitty lives they're living and stubbornly refusing to accept that they created that crap themselves. Regardless of the story, the truth remains the same: they're lying to themselves and refuse to accept the inescapable reality of personal accountability.

I know this because I was there too. Because I had told myself the same bullshit story since puberty, when my face was plastered with pimples. These imaginary stories in your head aren't telling you the truth and what's worse is that they tell you the same bullshit lies over and over until you end up believing them. And when that happens, those stories become your reality and slowly but surely, you inevitably end up living a lie.

You are more than capable of changing your life for the better. And if you refuse to change your stubborn ways and continue resisting the obvious need to, then the script of your life's story will stay the same and continue to suck balls. If nothing changes, indeed, nothing changes.

Let me dispel the myth of perfection by stating, for a fact, that there isn't a single person on God's green earth who doesn't feel flawed or imperfect, or who hasn't fucked up in some way, shape, or form. No one is perfect, dude. I repeat, **no one is perfect**. There is no such thing as achieving a state of perfection either. You will always be growing, no matter what you overcome or how polished you get.

You think you're fucked up? Puh-lease! You think your life is fucked? Hold my beer. You don't think you're capable of change? C'mon, man!! There's not much you can't come back from, brother. There isn't much people won't forgive you for. By no means are you the most fucked up person in the world nor have you had the most fucked up thing done *to* you. And in a bizarre way, that is an encouraging thought.

I felt like the biggest fuck up out there until I went to a group retreat in 2015 and 30 men and women stood up and told everyone their deepest secrets – the worst thing they'd ever done and the worst thing they'd ever gone through. That exercise was an eye-opener for me but also a comfort because it was clear as day that I wasn't alone in feeling that way. That I wasn't the only one who was fucked up.

My father used to say that if 20 people stood in a circle and each person put their problems in the middle then took a step back, folks would be fighting each other just to get their *own* problems back.

In order to create the firm foundation of change you must first understand that having fucked up in the past doesn't mean there's something permanently wrong with you. It's all about perspective.

The great thing is that there are tons of resources out there in the form of books (like this one), podcasts and blogs, created by people who've not only gone through what you're going through now, they actually got through it.

I just wanted to let you know that although you may feel fucked up, trust me my man, you are not the only one. And even if you do, nothing is preventing you from creating something different. You have everything you need to make your tomorrow better than your yesterday. So no more excuses, alright?

Remember, excuses are like assholes: everyone's got one and they all smell like shit. You can have results or excuses but you can't have both. Choose results, brother.

Accept Thy Self

The worst loneliness is not to be comfortable with yourself.
—Mark Twain

Because one believes in oneself, one doesn't try to convince others. Because one is content with oneself, one doesn't need others' approval. Because one accepts oneself, the whole world accepts him or her.
—Lao Tzu

A few weeks before this book was finished, I decided to go camping up in the picturesque Wasatch Mountains – above and away from the din of Salt Lake Valley – where I consciously consumed a "heroic dose" of mushroom tea. About 45 minutes into my journey, the five-plus grams of magic mushrooms began taking full effect and suddenly I found myself in familiar territory, where I was floating down the psychedelic-induced rabbit hole, leading to the untapped recesses of the mind.

As I sat around the campfire enjoying the fledgling stages of my journey – watching with wonderment how the flames danced, rose, and disappeared into the dark, starlit canopy above – I did what I always do when it comes to consuming mushrooms: I simply surrendered to the fungi's will. That's when it hit me in my head, heart and soul and I had what can only be described as an epiphany or a "Divine Download" from God.

I've had an incredibly difficult time accepting me for me. My whole life I've desperately tried to gain others' acceptance while refusing to accept myself for who I actually am. I've obsessed about what other people think of me. I've done everything to win people's favor, even if it meant losing favor with myself.

But that night – the night I surrendered to the mushrooms – I put an end to that shit, once and for all and realized that it's okay to be me. It's okay that I fucked up. It's okay that I'm not where I thought I'd be. It's okay to be Bryce Trevor Arnett. It was like I finally received permission **to just be me**!

It was like God gave me the thumbs up to stop caring about being accepted by others, to quit worrying about what others think of me, to start focusing on accepting me for me, and to stop giving a shit what anyone thinks - especially those random stranger dipshits on the road or in the store or some social media troll lurking on the internet.

That's when it also hit me that I was on the right path with my work in wanting to serve and support men who struggle with alcohol addiction, depression, suicide, and/or mental health. Self-acceptance is grounding and transformational, brother. Accept yourself. This means accepting everything that has happened in your life and everything that is happening in it right now. That means accepting and understanding that *you* played a role in all of it.

Maybe you were the victim in one of the chapters of your life's story. Maybe you were the villain. Maybe you were the hero. And just because you've played a certain role, that doesn't mean you have to continue casting yourself in that role; you can exit stage left at any moment you want.

Walk off the stage filled with conformists and sheep. Close that particular chapter of your life and begin writing a new one where you are centerstage, where you, my man, are the fucking rockstar. Because you are, brother. And self-acceptance will give you the foundation you need to believe it and start living it.

So you'd better start accepting that which I already know to be true about you. That you, my dear brother, are perfect, whole and complete just the way you are. Accept thy self.

Conclusion

A journey of a thousand miles begins with a single step.
—*Confucius*

The first step out of hell is always the hardest. And sometimes just taking a single step forward in a positive direction – no matter how small or insignificant that baby step might be or seem – requires Herculean fucking effort. Sometimes that's all you can do in a day. It's all you got. And if that's where you're at right now, then that's what **you fucking do.**

I've been there so many times before, myself, so you and I both know that if you haven't been in a place where it feels like all hope is lost, then you have **zero** fucking clue how debilitating that level of misery can truly be. So don't you **dare** listen to what anyone else tells you to the contrary, alright? Fuck. Them.

I am living proof that you can turn your life around just by changing your attitude, which is to say by changing your mindset. I hated me so much that I wished death upon myself every night for a solid decade there like I was blowing out candles atop a *Groundhog Day*-cake made from crap.

And even now as I sit here at 40 years young, I'm not entirely sure how I made it through it all or how I managed to survive... me. Nevertheless, I am eternally grateful that I experienced those fresh levels of hell because it reaffirmed my passion and purpose in life, which is helping men help themselves out of the same or similar hell.

But I didn't do it on a dime either. broheim. It took me that first year of my sobriety just to learn how to stop moving backwards altogether, force myself to turnabout, and teach myself how to put one foot before the other. I had to learn how to fucking *walk* again.

As I come up on my third year of sobriety – my sober-date is 1/22/20, BTW – and finally put this book to rest and close that old bullshit story of my life – I am only *now* seeing the benefits of taking hundreds if not thousands of steps from that initial, incredibly uncomfortable, super scary first step I made the day I decided to stop drinking and start living. Brother, I know you can do it too. And I want to help you as much as humanly fucking possible but I *can't* take that step for you.

I can't make you stop drinking, smoking, doing drugs, watching porn, stealing, lying, cheating, or anything else you're doing that's not serving you or your higher purpose in this life. And neither can anyone else. That's all on you, homie.

You might be your own worst enemy but you can also be your biggest fan and ultimate support system. You are the answer to everything, brother. No one is coming to save you. Not your mom or dad. Not your wife or girlfriend. Not Jesus, Buddha, Zeus, who or whatever it is you believe in or don't, the fact remains the same so get used to saying it to yourself now: no one is coming to save me but... me.

What makes me qualified to teach men about the topics I wrote about in this book is that I am as successful as it gets when it comes to getting back up again. I'm resilient as fuck! And this book is proof that I got back up at least one more time.

This book is proof that miracles are real. It's a miracle I survived long enough to write it, and it's a miracle I finished it because time and time again I wanted to give up and give in.

I had impostor syndrome like a motherfucker. Like, "Who the hell am I to impart wisdom on other men?" But at some point, I just had to punch that fucker in the mouth, shut his negative ass up, sit down and grind my way through it. And it was a grind, brother. I fought against my old story the whole way.

I love helping and serving others. It's the best drug I've ever done. And if this book has had any impact on your life, I'd love to hear about it. I'd love to connect with you on social media so please reach out, especially if you're down in the dumps. I'll give you a hand up, brother. I'll show you how to get there.

I'll leave you with a passage from the book that not only inspired me to write mine but more importantly, inspired me to change my life by changing my mind alone. It should be required reading for everyone, and I definitely recommend it so grab a copy ASAP. It's by 19th Century British philosopher James Allen, and he wrote *As a Man Thinketh*.

And since he's been dead for over a hundred years, I doubt he'll mind if I borrow the final paragraph from his timelessly profound book and share it with you:

"Tempest-tossed souls, wherever ye may be, under whatsoever conditions ye may live, know this – in the ocean of life isles of Blessedness are smiling, and the sunny shore of your ideal awaits your coming. Keep your hand firmly upon the helm of thought. In the bark of yourself reclines the commanding Master; He does but sleep; wake Him. Self-control is strength; Right Thought is mastery; Calmness is power. Say unto your heart, 'Peace, be still!'"

Thanks again for reading my book. I hope our paths connect one day soon. Be well, brother. I'm rooting for you the whole fucking way!

Much Love,

Bryce

About the Author

Bryce Arnett is a father, husband, author, speaker, mentor, and on an indefatigable mission to support struggling men all around the globe.

He lives a blissfully unsatisfied life with his amazing family, somewhere along the foothills of the Wasatch Mountains.

To see what he's currently up to, please follow Bryce on social media or contact him at www.brycearnett.com

Instagram: @thebrycearnett
Facebook: @brycearnett